THE CALGARY STAMPEDE

PRAIRIE POSTCARDS PC006277

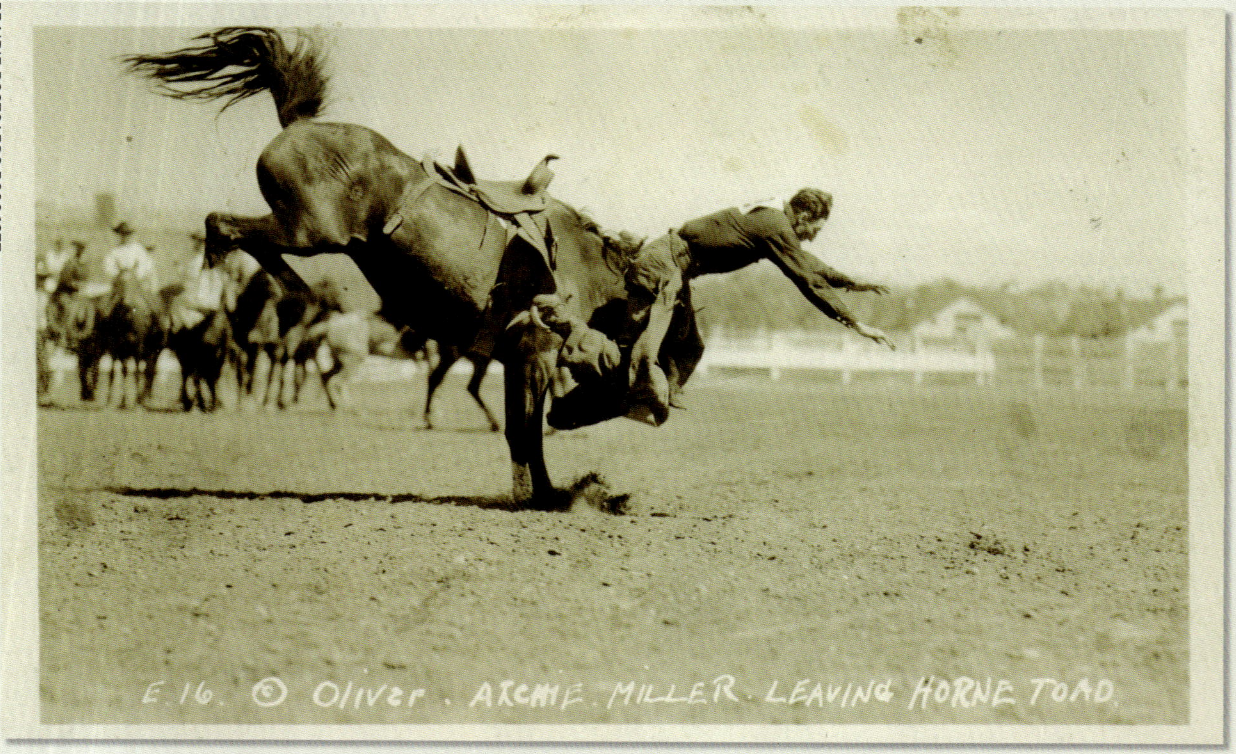

Archie Miller experiences a sudden upending from Horne Toad.
Photographer W.J. Oliver captured just the right moment.

THE CALGARY STAMPEDE

A Collection of Vintage Postcards

KEN TINGLEY

RMB
Victoria Vancouver Calgary

Rocky Mountain Books
www.rmbooks.com

Library and Archives Canada Cataloguing in Publication

Tingley, Kenneth W. (Kenneth Wayne), 1947-
The Calgary Stampede : a century of vintage postcards / Ken Tingley.

Includes bibliographical references and index.
ISBN 978-1-927330-00-5

1. Calgary Stampede—Alberta—Calgary—History—Pictorial works. 2. Calgary (Alta.)—History—Pictorial works. 3. Postcards—Alberta—Calgary. I. Title.

GV1834.56.C22T55 2012 791.8'4097123380222
C2011-908382-5

Front cover photo: Prairie Postcards PC006281. Paddy Ryan, one of the many US cowboys to compete in Calgary, riding Barnacle Bill in 1930. Ryan was from Ismay, Montana.

Printed in Canada

Rocky Mountain Books acknowledges the financial support for its publishing program from the Government of Canada through the Canada Book Fund (CBF) and the Canada Council for the Arts, and from the province of British Columbia through the British Columbia Arts Council and the Book Publishing Tax Credit.

Canadian Heritage Patrimoine canadien

Canada Council for the Arts Conseil des Arts du Canada

British Columbia Arts Council

This book was produced using FSC®-certified, acid-free paper, processed chlorine free and printed with vegetable-based inks.

FSC MIX Paper from responsible sources FSC® C016245

The foresight of the University of Alberta Libraries in acquiring the massive postcard collection from which the images in this book are drawn is greatly appreciated. Special thanks to Robert Desmarais, Merrill Distad, Sharon Farnel and Jeff Papineau for their support and advice.

PRAIRIE POSTCARDS PC006312

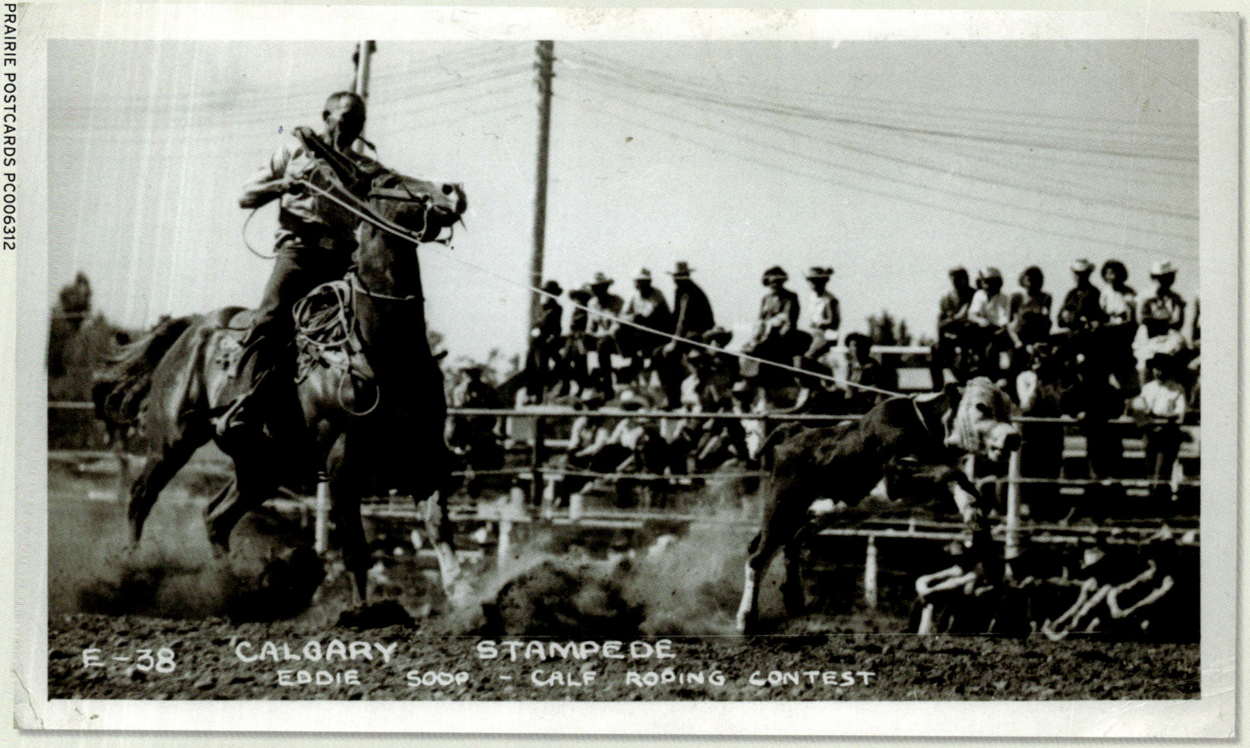

Eddie Soop calf roping at the 1951 Calgary Stampede, in another action-packed McDermid postcard

CONTENTS

ROOTS OF THE CALGARY STAMPEDE

The roots of Stampede run deep in Alberta history. Trace them back and they tell the story of a long struggle to get the show off the ground. Cattle, horses, cowboys, cowgirls, "Indians," homesteaders, ranchers – all had been a part of southern Alberta from its early territorial days. But it took almost three decades of energetic efforts to bring together the key elements of a unique place and culture into the special experience that is known around the world today as the Calgary Stampede.

The southwesterly section of what at the time was called the North-Western Territory had for many years been viewed as Blackfoot and buffalo country. But fairly soon after the vast expanse was transferred from the Hudson's Bay Company to the new Dominion of Canada during 1869 and '70, that view was supplanted in the popular imagination by the image of a vast cattle range. Cattle trails had been pushing the North American ranching frontier westward and northward out of Texas in the years following the US Civil War. The first cattle drive crossed the Medicine Line into Canada in 1876, when US cowboys brought a herd to the Fort Macleod district to feed the treaty "Indians" camped there.

Other cattle drives followed, a trend greatly accelerated in 1881 when the Canadian government passed regulations allowing, and encouraging, cattlemen to lease up to 100,000 acres of land for a mere one cent per acre per year, for up to 21 years. These early ranchers were obliged to stock their ranges with one cow for every ten acres within three years in order to keep their vast spreads of virtually free grazing land. Although this would later be reduced to one cow per twenty acres to prevent overgrazing, it was clear that the big ranching leaseholders would need many cattle to become established. One estimate claimed there were more than 75,000 along the Bow River by 1884, the year the Calgary agricultural fair was first planned, including both Texas longhorns and the crossbred cattle brought in from the Pacific Northwest.

Lord Argyll, Marquess of Lorne, who was Governor General of Canada from 1878 to 1883,

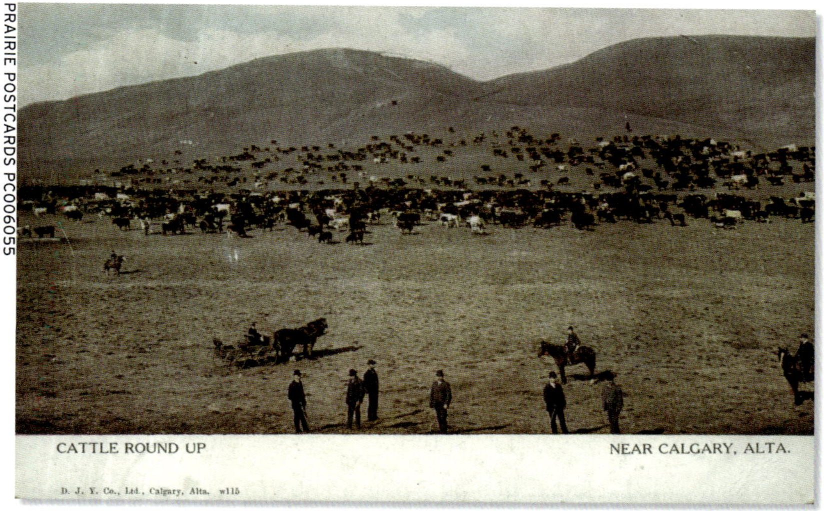

PRAIRIE POSTCARDS PC006055

This early cattle roundup scene, published by D.J.Y. & Co. Ltd. of Calgary and printed by Warwick Bros. & Rutter Ltd. of Toronto, was mailed during the first Calgary Stampede, in 1912.

"Had big day today," wrote the correspondent on the back of the card. "Took in the 'Stampede' never saw anything like it before."

made a famous trip across the North-Western Territory in the pivotal year of 1881. His enthusiastic endorsement of the land and its potential, conveyed to international readers by the contingent of British journalists that accompanied him, encouraged further investment in western ranching. By this time Buffalo Bill Cody's Wild West Shows also were introducing "the West" to eager British and European fans.

The purpose that later developed into the Calgary Exhibition & Stampede is almost as old as Calgary itself. When the Canadian Pacific Railway reached the confluence of the Bow and Elbow rivers in 1883, a little settlement grew up near the North-West Mounted Police post that had been established at Fort Calgary in 1875. Interest in development and speculation in the North-Western Territory was at one of its low points at the time, and the reputation of the Calgary district was in danger of suffering in the perpetual argument about whether it was a potential Garden of Eden, or the dry and desolate land declared by John Palliser when he had explored the West twenty-five years before.

Thomas Braden, editor of the *Calgary Herald*, is credited with first addressing the problem when, on August 6, 1884, he suggested the idea of an agricultural fair to spread the word that the local crops were doing phenomenally well that year. The tiny, ramshackle settlement strung along the railway tracks needed just such a fair to convince doubting Thomases and "knockers" in eastern Canada that Calgary had a lot to offer settlers and investors.

The Calgary & District Agricultural Society was established in 1884 to fulfill this goal. It succeeded in convincing the CPR to provide a railway demonstration car to take district crops east to convince skeptics in Ontario, Quebec and the Maritimes of the agricultural potential of the North-West during the fall and winter of 1884–85. Such displays became a part of CPR promotion nationally and internationally after this first effort proved successful. Also in 1884, Colonel James Walker, one of the principal promoters of a Calgary fair, convinced

A.M. Burgess, the federal deputy minister of agriculture, to provide 94 acres along the Elbow River south of the Calgary settlement. The plan was to use this land as the fairgrounds, although negotiations would not be completed until 1888.

Meanwhile, the Calgary fair struggled to get on its feet. With the completion of the CPR transcontinental line spurring the growth of Calgary, the first fair finally was held October 19 and 20, 1886, with agricultural and mercantile exhibits and handicrafts displayed in the Star skating rink. Despite the district's still small population and a dearth of entries, not to mention an early blizzard, some five hundred people attended this inaugural effort. However, the terrible winter of 1886–87, which would become notorious in western Canadian and US high plains history, devastated the cattle herds of the West. The summer of 1887, with its heat and drought, also plagued homesteaders. All in all, enthusiasm for the glories of western farming and ranching was already beginning to flag by the time the 1887 fair opened.

When the Crown land along the Elbow, at what would be called Victoria Park, was finally sold to the agricultural society in 1888, prospects looked a bit more optimistic for a brief time. In 1889 the society's board of directors obtained a mortgage as soon as the deed was registered for the exhibition grounds, and used the resulting funds to build its first racetrack, cattle sheds and exhibition building. Although the 1890 exhibition had to be postponed due to very heavy rain, and the 1895 fair cancelled when a devastating blizzard struck, the events held during the rest of the early 1890s did moderately well despite declines in wheat prices and a stagnating western economy.

With the completion of the Calgary & Edmonton Railway in 1891, Calgary became a distribution centre for the entire region, from Fort Macleod near the US border to Edmonton, boosting its prosperity. The C & E also made it easier for many more people to attend the fairs in Calgary. However, by 1895 both the fair and its sustaining society were no longer active. That year, the vicious early winter weather destroyed a promising bumper crop in the territories, and all efforts that fall had to be directed toward salvaging any crops that could be saved. Although Victoria Park was abandoned as an exhibition ground for a while, some district communities continued to hold their own small agricultural fairs. However, the government of Prime Minister Wilfrid Laurier, under his energetic Minister of the Interior, Clifford Sifton, began to attract more immigration and investment to the North-West after 1896, despite the fact that the western agricultural economy continued to languish.

During 1899 Arthur G. Wolley-Dod promoted the Inter-Western Pacific Exhibition Company, an initiative that would prove to be central to the next phase in the development of a Calgary fair. The IWPE exposition would return to Victoria Park, which had fallen into the hands of R.B. Bennett when the board that governed the facility for the Calgary & District Agricultural Society defaulted on its mortgage. Mounted in September that year, Wolley-Dod's exhibition was sufficiently successful to indicate the need for improved facilities for the future, especially an adequate grandstand. Another fair followed in 1900.

In March 1901 IWPE purchased the grounds from Bennett, and in 1903 it was decided to co-operate with the Calgary Board of Trade to hire C.W. Peterson as a joint manager to direct their activities, along with his assistant Ernest L. (Ernie) Richardson, thus cementing the relationship between the fair and the Calgary business community. Peterson had been one of the founders of the Territorial Livestock Association in 1900, and would ensure that a strong connection was established with the cattle breeders, whose shows would become an important part of the exhibition. Ernie Richardson, who would remain central to Stampede development until his retirement in 1940, replaced Peterson in 1907. The exhibition would remain on a more consistent, organized footing after the decision to hire Peterson and Richardson.

PRAIRIE POSTCARDS PC009889

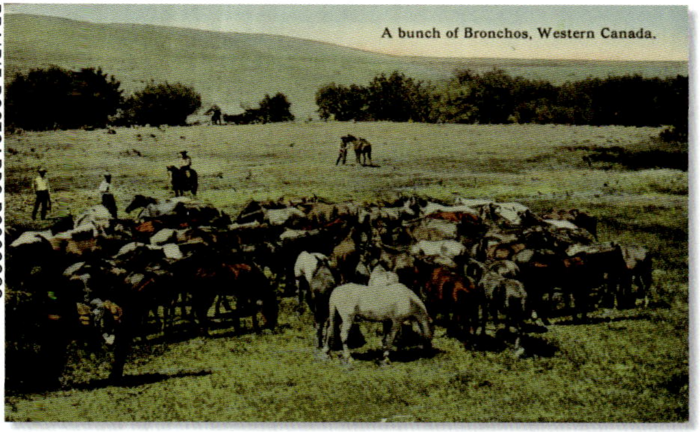

Bloom Brothers of Winnipeg published this scene of "a bunch of Bronchos" just before the First World War. Postmarked May 13, 1913, this C.T. Photochrom card promoted the upcoming Winnipeg Stampede later that summer. Postcards like this reflect the connection of the Stampede to its source of stock.

PRAIRIE POSTCARDS PC023445

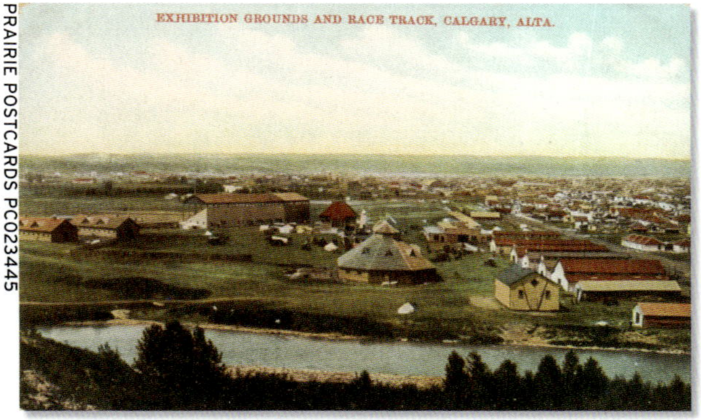

The Calgary Exhibition Grounds and racetrack shortly after completion of the barns.

After the consistently disastrous weather of the autumns through the 1890s, efforts were made to move the exhibition from fall to summer. The 1903 fair was held in July, but still the constant nemesis of bad weather seemed to conspire against the new idea just as it had done during most of the early exhibitions. Heavy rains closed the roads around the city, reducing gate receipts, but nevertheless the event would continue to be held during July after 1903. Under Peterson, improvements were made to accommodate all events at Victoria Park rather than use other, downtown venues as well. In 1904 the price of admission was reduced from fifty cents to a quarter, greatly increasing attendance during a three-day event and setting a trend for low ticket prices that would last for many years. Also in 1904, many purely entertainment acts were added, including trick riding, wild-horse races and the first hot-air balloonist to amaze the crowds.

The Dominion Exhibition, launched in Toronto in 1903, was held in different Canadian cities in succeeding years, and when it came to Calgary in 1908 it gave the homegrown fair a tremendous boost. Through this prestigious show the federal government aimed to encourage improvement in the quality of regional farm production through highlighting the best practices and breeds. Ernie Richardson, the new manager of the Calgary Exhibition, with the assistance of I.S.G. VanWart, the Calgary exhibition president, organized a tremendous show. Alberta was less than two years old when it was decided to hold the Dominion Exhibition in Calgary. "In a way it was like a consolation prize that was awarded to Calgary for losing both the provincial capital and the University of Alberta to Edmonton," observed James Gray in his history of the Calgary Exhibition & Stampede, "and Calgary made the most of it."

PRAIRIE POSTCARDS PC006090

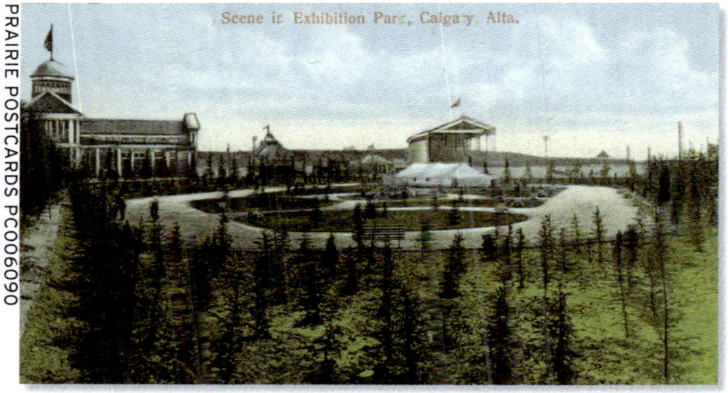

This tinted postcard, published by L.C. Wilson of Calgary, is an early view of Exhibition Park, showing the Grandstand, Racetrack and Industrial Building in about 1908.

Relief followed fears that the worst winter since the infamous one of 1886–87, plus a coal shortage on the prairies, would dampen enthusiasm for the

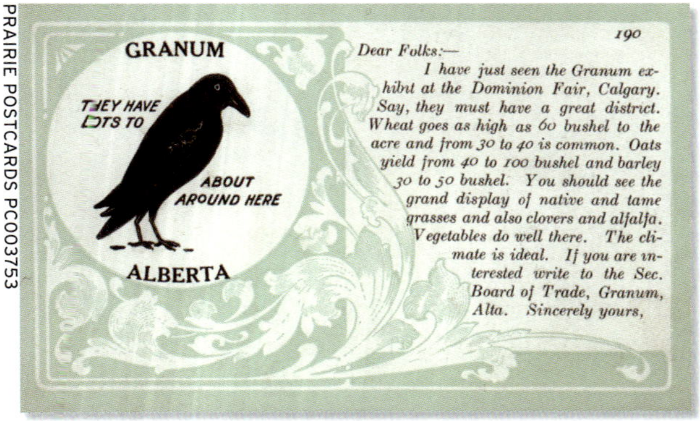

PRAIRIE POSTCARDS PC003753

A Granum, Alberta, advertising card, part of a common genre at the time. The motto "They have lots to [crow] about around here" heralds the town's participation in the 1908 Dominion Fair at Calgary.

big event. But hard work by the IWPE company throughout the former North-Western Territory resulted in an impressive number of entrants from far and wide for the events held between June 29 and July 9, 1908.

On that Dominion Day, a "historical pageant" (parade) was held, with local First Nations well represented in their traditional regalia. Despite opposition from the Department of Indian Affairs, concerned that such reminders of traditional indigenous lifestyle would undercut departmental efforts to inculcate agricultural values in their wards, many native people turned out for the big event. Rev. John McDougall, the pioneer missionary to the Stoney at Morley, organized such Indian entrants from 1908 until 1910, although the Temperance & Moral Reform League, political groups and churches almost unanimously opposed such activities. McDougall also organized an Indian Village located near the reconstructed trading post on the grounds. Political and business dignitaries and a lengthy procession of floats added to the colourful pageant, and this became the first of a permanent succession of Stampede parades.

Livestock and dog shows also entranced the crowds in 1908, while the Strobel dirigible flew by the grandstand several times, to the wonder of one and all, until a wind gust pushed it against the

PRAIRIE POSTCARDS PC006088

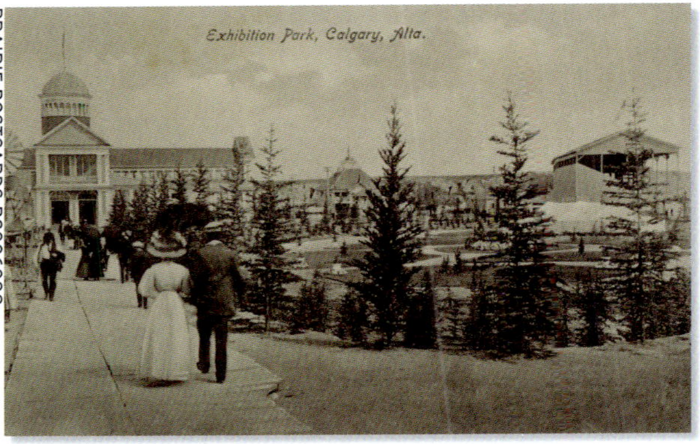

Calgary Exhibition Grounds with the Grandstand at right, the Industrial Building at left and a flower garden in the foreground, ca. 1910. Lane's Dominion Stores Ltd., with head office located in Calgary, held the copyright to this image. Bloom Brothers Co. of Minneapolis was the publisher.

grandstand on July 4 and the airship exploded and burned. That date also marked "American Day" at the fair, with a special trainload of people visiting from Spokane. The event was so successful that it led to further, similar excursions. Other Alberta newcomers from the United States and border towns also flocked to the show, initiating the special connection that has lasted ever since. Over 100,000 attended "Western Canada's Greatest Fair," and Calgary's hotels and restaurants were crowded to bursting.

Encouraged by the success of the 1908 event, the board of directors decided to duplicate their success at the Alberta Provincial Exhibition, held in Calgary in 1909. The Calgary Exhibition had now reached the big time and wanted the world to know about it. It co-operated with the CPR to produce a promotional film that year, featuring the colourful historical pageant along with the western railway hotels. The Provincial Exhibition was distinguished by the biggest art show ever held in the West (mounted by the federal Minister of Agriculture, since the National Art Gallery, strangely, came under his portfolio), a motorcycle act, the C.W. Parker carnival and the A.G. Barnes animal circus. Heavy July rains reduced attendance for several years after this, but such innovations and a growing local population continued to sustain the show. Art exhibitions would become a recurring part of the Calgary exhibitions, with the Royal College of Art and Alberta artists like Roland Gissing showing their landscapes in 1934.

By 1910 it was felt that the Calgary event had grown to the point that a new name should be chosen, and the Calgary Industrial Exhibition Co. came into being. The new name was hardly a ringing endorsement of the community's rural and ranching roots. In 1911 the exhibition undertook construction of the enormous Victoria Arena, a horse show and livestock facility that could seat three thousand and would become the all-season venue for the city. Calgarians began to wonder which way their community image would develop. Should the summer fair continue to largely focus on its western ranching and farming heritage, or should it develop a more "industrial" perspective in keeping with emerging aspirations for a diversified urban economy?

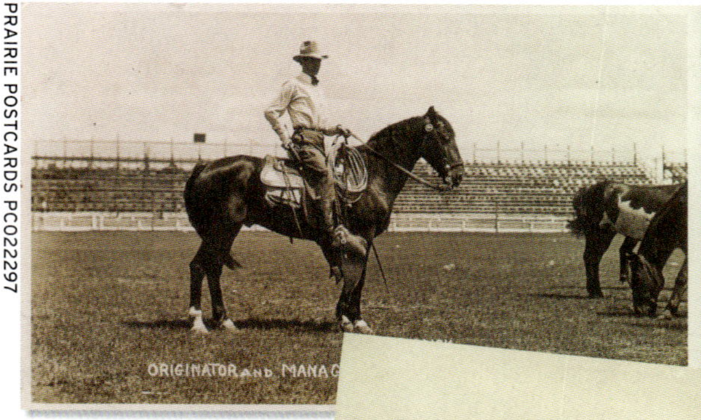

PRAIRIE POSTCARDS PC022297

A mounted Guy Weadick at the Winnipeg Dominion Exhibition in 1913.

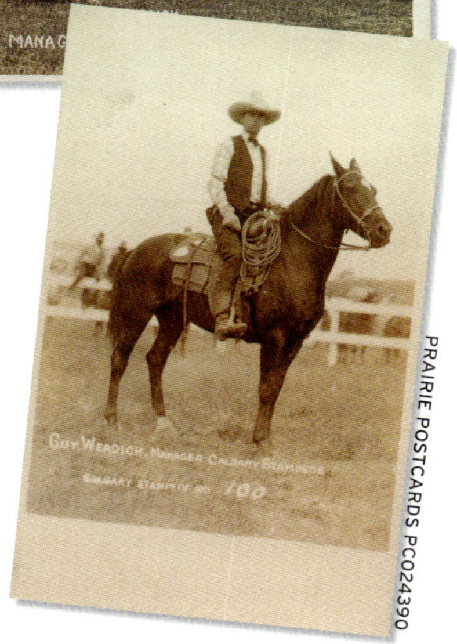

PRAIRIE POSTCARDS PC024390

Guy Weadick, the inventive force behind the Stampede's early success, and one of its greatest managers.

Guy Weadick came along at an opportune moment and left his permanent mark not only on the history of Calgary but on the way the whole world would perceive the city from then on. Weadick was a working cowboy who had moved into the emerging rodeo circuit in the early 1900s. He had worked on Alberta's McIntyre Ranch in 1904 and represented the legendary black "bulldogger" Bill Pickett when he performed at the 1905 Calgary grandstand show.

Weadick had been in Calgary in 1908 at the great Dominion Exhibition, performing as a "trick roping" cowboy with the celebrated Miller Brothers 101 Ranch Wild West Show. While there he met H.C. McMullen, general livestock agent for the CPR, and proposed that they co-operate to stage a week-long rodeo. When the Calgary Industrial Exhibition balked at the idea, McMullen approached rancher George Lane, who brought in industrialist Pat Burns and politician A.J. McLean. Brewery magnate A.E. Cross came on board too, and the four of them arranged the $100,000 worth of financing (the equivalent of nearly $2-million today) that was needed to get the first Calgary Stampede established. "The Big Four," as they came to be known, are still remembered.

George Lane (1856–1925), was a US-born politician and rancher, best known as the foreman at the renowned Bar U Ranch. He left the Bar U in 1887 and became a large-scale cattle buyer so successful that he returned and bought the Bar U and several other spreads as well. Realizing that the spread of settlement on the prairies would result in thousands of farmers needing large numbers of draft horses, Lane built the Bar U into the largest purebred Percheron breeder in the world. He was one of the founding members of the Western Stock Growers' Association and the Cattlemen's Protective Association. Elected to the Alberta legislature in 1913, Lane resigned shortly afterward to allow a defeated cabinet minister to regain a seat. After Lane's death, the Bar U was bought by Pat Burns.

Patrick Burns (1856–1937) was a rancher, businessman, senator and philanthropist and one of the wealthiest Canadians of his time. Born in Ontario, he had already made his first fortune by the time he moved to Calgary in 1890. He established his first important slaughterhouse in the city in 1898, followed by other large western packing plants. P. Burns & Co. (later called Burns Foods) became western Canada's largest meatpacking company and Burns turned to ranching on a large scale. Appointed to the Senate in 1931 by his close friend Prime Minister R.B. Bennett, Burns sat as an independent until he resigned for health reasons in 1936. After his death, the tax alone on his estate was enough to offset a provincial deficit and balance the budget.

The third member of the Big Four, A.J. (Archie) McLean (1860–1933), also was a cattleman and politician. Born in Ontario in 1860, McLean moved to what is now Alberta to work as a ranch hand, and soon became manager of the vast CY spread near present-day Taber, building it into one of the largest growers of cattle for export. First elected to the Alberta legislature in 1909, for the Lethbridge constituency, he later served as minister of municipal affairs and minister of public works. McLean left politics in 1921 to return to ranching. At his death, the Fort Macleod *Gazette* described his memorial service as being "probably the largest funeral ever held in southern Alberta."

The remaining member of the Big Four was Alfred Ernest Cross (1861–1932), also a politician and rancher, but perhaps best known as a brewer. Born in Montreal and trained as a veterinarian, he moved west in 1884 to work on a ranch near Cochrane, Alberta. Only two years later Cross founded the A7 Ranche, near what is now Nanton. In 1891 he established the Calgary Brewing & Malting Company, the first brewery in the North-Western Territory. Cross entered provincial politics in 1898, when he was elected to represent East Calgary on the territorial council. In addition to his pivotal role in financing the first Calgary Stampede, Cross served as a director and president of the Calgary General Hospital, president of the

PRAIRIE POSTCARDS PC006163

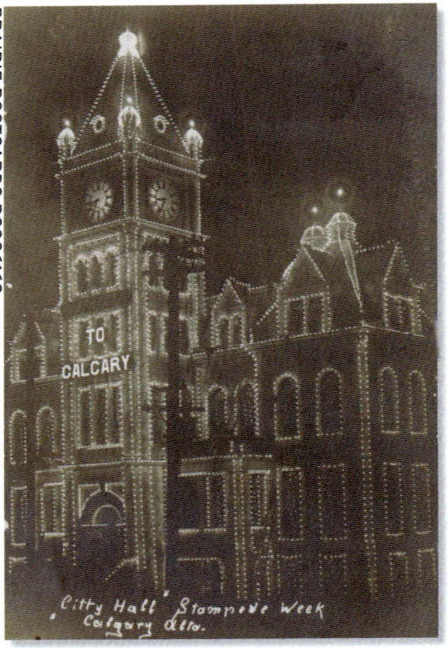

Calgary City Hall was lit up like a Christmas tree for the first Stampede. The writing on the reverse of this postcard notes that "the Duke of Connaught had dinner with six hundred cow boys [sic] – mostly Yankies [sic]... ."

PRAIRIE POSTCARDS PC002203

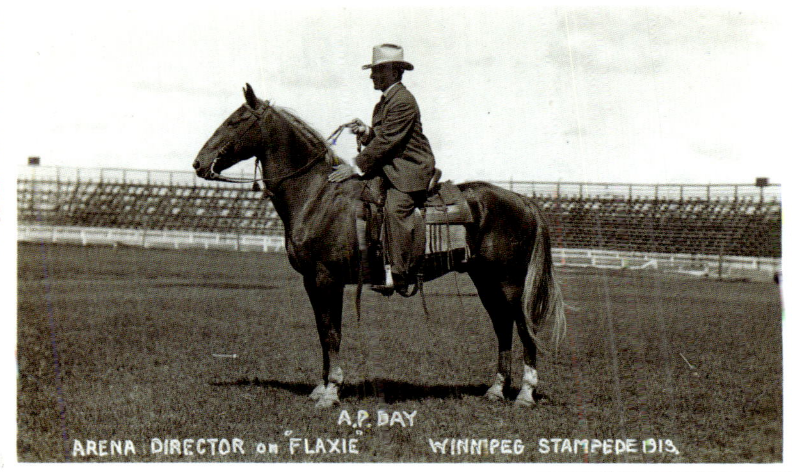

A.P. Day, the arena director, mounted on Flaxie at the 1913 Winnipeg Stampede. The Lyall Commercial Photo Co. produced this postcard.

Alberta Exhibition Association and president of the Calgary Board of Trade.

Once the Big Four had put up the seed money, Weadick began touring North America to sign people up for the first Stampede. He seemed to know virtually everyone in the rodeo business, and by March 1912 he had successfully booked many famous performers and

PRAIRIE POSTCARDS PC018801

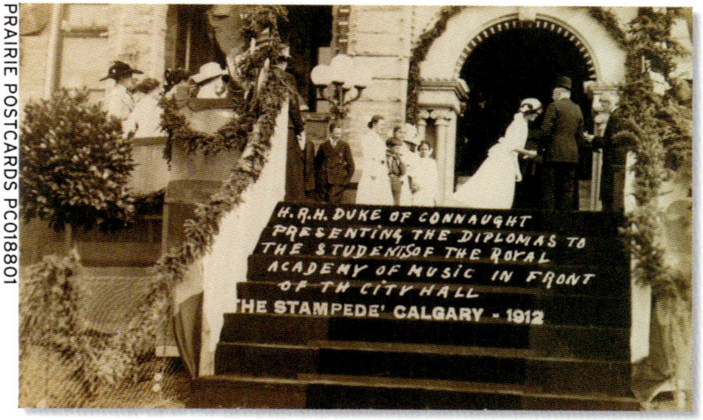

At the outset of the 1912 Stampede, HRH Prince Arthur, Duke of Connaught and Strathearn and Governor General of Canada, presented graduation diplomas to students of the Royal Academy of Canada at the entrance of Calgary City Hall. Such images reassured Calgarians that their city had become a significant urban centre, and were widely distributed through postcards like this one.

competitors. Another early Stampede organizer, Medicine Hat rancher A.P. Day, supplied much of the livestock and became the first arena director. Weadick even persuaded legendary western artists Charlie Russell and Ed Borein to come to town and show their paintings.

The inaugural 1912 show was extended two days to accommodate a visit by Governor General the Duke of Connaught, for whom a special welcome arch was constructed in the fashion of the day and who viewed the excitement from a special "royal box" in the grandstand.

Royal and vice-regal visits have been an important part of Stampede history throughout its first century. The enormously popular Prince of Wales, who loved Alberta so much that he purchased the EP Ranch near Pekisko in 1919, presented a special trophy to bronc rider Pete Vandermeer during the 1923 Stampede. The Prince of Wales trophy has been a part of the Stampede tradition ever since. In 1928 Viscount and Lady Willingdon spent the week in Calgary, making appearances at the

Stampede. King George VI and Queen Elizabeth attended on June 26, 1939, during their famous prewar tour of North America. Princess Elizabeth and the Duke of Edinburgh attended in 1951 and again in 1959 soon after the beginning of the new Elizabethan Age. Elizabeth and Phillip returned in 1973 and 1990 and again in 2005 for the Alberta Centennial celebrations. In 1977 Prince Charles and Prince Andrew attended the Stampede during centennial celebrations commemorating the signing of Treaty 7 with six First Nations.

In 1912, however, First Nations participation in the first Stampede was still a contentious issue, just as it had been for the Calgary Exhibition in 1908. The Department of Indian Affairs requested that the Duke of Connaught exercise his influence to keep the "Indians" on their reserves during harvesting and haying. Connaught conveyed his refusal by way of an aide-de-camp. Efforts were also made to use the RNWMP to keep the Blackfoot, Sarcee and Stoney at home, but police superintendent R.B. Deane too refused. It took the intervention of such worthies as Senator James Lougheed and Calgary's Member of Parliament, R.B. Bennett, to persuade Indian Affairs to reverse its strong opposition. Eventually the Minister of Indian Affairs, Robert Rogers, instructed southern Alberta reserve personnel to aid in bringing their charges to Calgary for the Stampede. The Blood rider Tom Three Persons was the sole Canadian contestant to win in rodeo that year, taking the bucking title by

PRAIRIE POSTCARDS PC006125

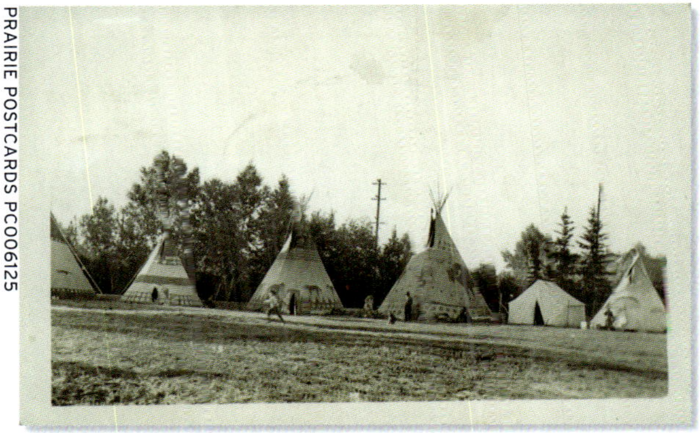

The Calgary Stampede Indian Village about 1933.

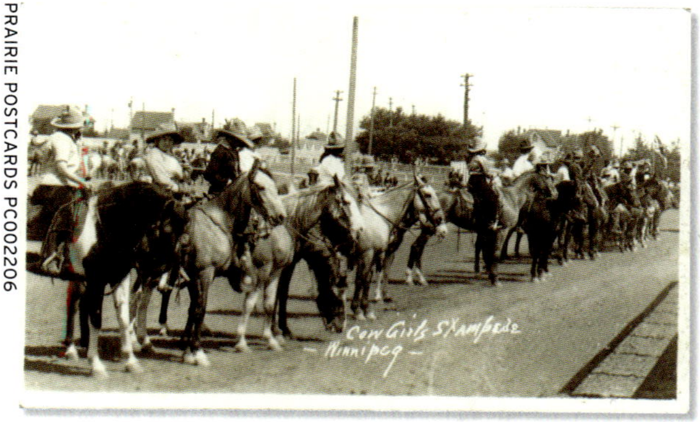

PRAIRIE POSTCARDS PC002206

Cowgirls have been part of the Calgary Stampede, and of its various prairie counterparts, from their beginnings. Here, a group of cowgirls line up at the 1913 Winnipeg Stampede.

riding an infamous bronc named Cyclone into the ground. The win launched Three Persons to fame and he went on to become a successful rancher and a legendary part of Alberta history. From that year on, the "Indian" presence was well established as part of the vibrant spectacle of Stampede.

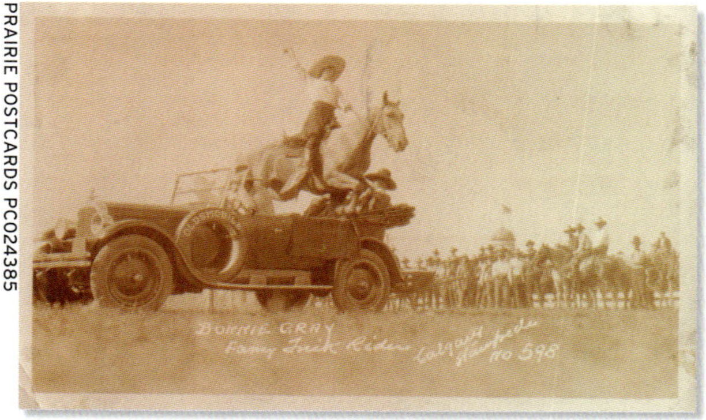

PRAIRIE POSTCARDS PC024385

Bonnie Gray, fancy trick rider, jumps her mount over a well-advertised Oldsmobile.

Like the old Buffalo Bill Wild West Show, Weadick's vision extended to a hundred imported American Indians, additional Mexican riders and a sensational array of American cowboys. Huge prizes attracted attention from every corner of the rodeo world. The champion bronc rider, steer wrestler and calf roper each won a thousand dollars, a new saddle and a silver belt buckle. The

Labour Day parade that started the first Stampede was a huge success, and later at the show, cowgirls amazed the grandstand crowds with their "fancy riding" and trick roping. Women were a big part of the Stampede from the beginning, and Alberta McMullen, daughter of H.C. McMullen, was named the first all-round Canadian cowgirl in 1912.

There were quite a few glitches at the first Stampede. Since there were no chutes yet, broncs had to be "snubbed" so that riders could mount "free form." "The ride might take the bucker from one end of the infield to the other," as James Gray notes, "for the horse had to be ridden, sometimes for several minutes, until it ceased to buck." Lack of organization resulted in the 1912 events petering out as the sun set. Rain began to mire things down the second day. A thunderstorm cast its pall on the day when Governor General Connaught and his party attended. Bulldogged longhorns provided a bloody spectacle when their horns were torn out, a foretaste of later concerns about animal cruelty. Mostly, disappointment centred on the fact that there would be no profit from the first show.

Despite the fundamental failure of the first Stampede, the seed had been sown and would later come to maturity. In 1913 a great plan was put in place to expand Victoria Park to include a Superintendent's Cottage, a new Grandstand for 11,000 spectators, a Manufacturers Building, Implement Building, Horse Barns, a Cattle Barn and a Sheep & Swine Building, as well as water and sewer connections, lighting, roads and sidewalks. However, the economic slump of 1913, followed by four years of global war, shut down these plans.

When the Great War broke out, the Calgary parades assumed a military bearing, with columns of uniformed men marching through the city. Katherine Stinson, the famous American aviatrix, visited in 1917 and 1918, although her performance was washed out by very heavy winds. Stinson would return successfully in 1919, but that was the year Captain Fred McCall crash-landed his aircraft on the midway, impaling it on the merry-go-

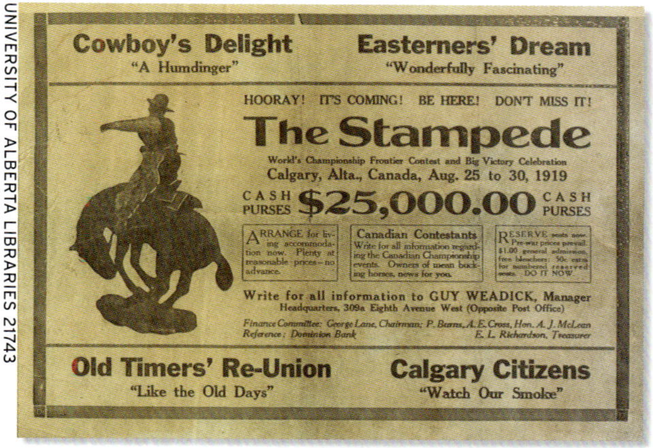

UNIVERSITY OF ALBERTA LIBRARIES 21743

The Stampede was poised to roll out again after the First World War, and challenged Calgarians to "watch our smoke" in 1919.

round. Still, McCall and "Wop" May thrilled the crowds with aerobatics. John Philip Sousa and his band also performed that year.

With the war and the terrible Spanish influenza pandemic over, the time seemed right to plan a new, bigger and better Stampede for 1919. That summer, Guy Weadick returned to announce an ambitious Calgary Victory Stampede for August 25–30, 1919. The old gang would organize it and the Big Four would underwrite it again. Although the date came during harvest, it would allow many cowboys to come north from the rodeo at Bozeman, Montana, to attend. This time, saddling chutes would be provided. Profits were to be handed on to the Great War Veterans Association, the Salvation Army and the YMCA. Everyone profited but the Stampede itself, which seems to have barely broken even. Merchants did quite well, though, and they began looking for related ways to attract people to Calgary.

A new generation of cowboys showed up at the Stampede after the First World War. Guy and Flo Weadick, on their US vaudeville tours, had met Yakima Canutt, a charismatic rodeo rider and western melodrama actor. Canutt and Tom Mix were replacing William S. Hart in the hearts of nickelodeon patrons. Weadick convinced Yakima and Kitty Canutt to attend the 1919 Stampede.

Kitty was a trick rider and fancy rider specializing in the spectacular, standing-up, two-horse Roman race. Yakima was attracted by the chance to ride an infamous "unrideable" horse named Fox, ranch-raised at Gleichen, Alberta. Although Canutt could not seem to draw Fox to ride, he demanded, after the other entrants had been thrown, that he be allowed to ride him, in the wake of rumours that the American rider was afraid to challenge the Canadian outlaw. "Fox literally turned himself inside out," wrote Calgary writer Fred Kennedy. "His angry squeals could be heard above the roar of the crowd. For eight jumps the American champion rode him 'straight up' and then on the ninth jump, Fox suddenly whipped back and sunfished and Canutt was long gone. Both horse and rider were cheered to the echo." American cowboys seemed to dominate the events that year.

Gradually the rodeo idea began to make a comeback. In 1920 Guy Weadick bought a dude ranch near Pekisko, Alberta, not far from the famous EP Ranch, and in 1921 Ernie Richardson convinced

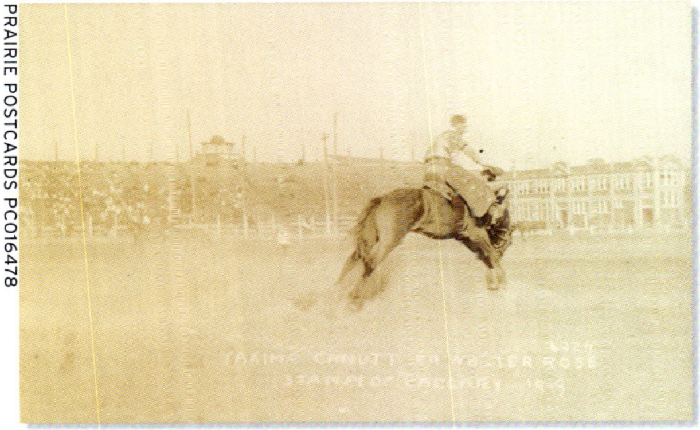

PRAIRIE POSTCARDS PC016478

Yakima Canutt's great ride of 1919.

Guy and Flo to perform trick riding and roping during the intermission of the evening Spring Horse Show. In 1922 the Weadicks added a miniature rodeo, which would inspire the cash-strapped directors to reconsider the value of a full rodeo. Richardson called Weadick back yet again in 1923 for the "Calgary Exhibition, Stampede & Buffalo Barbeque," with bison steaks provided by the federal government. This was the first real melding of

PRAIRIE POSTCARDS PC006110

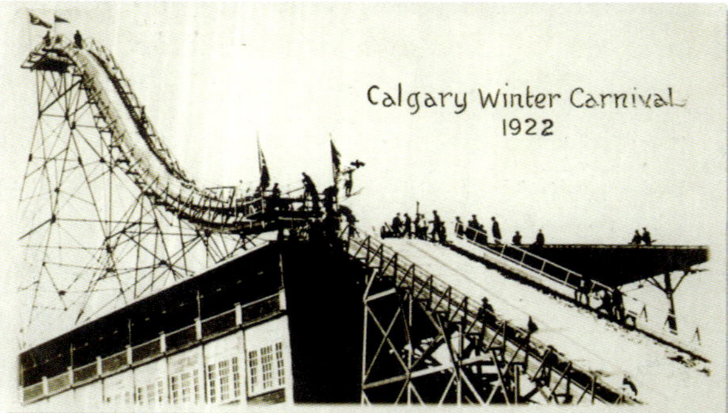

A ski jump was rigged to the roof of the Grandstand for the Calgary Winter Carnival in 1921, shown here the following year. This was a good example of diversification of Stampede grounds events.

exhibition and stampede, and Weadick was hired as Stampede manager between January and July to get the show back into full swing. In 1923, greater efforts were made to attract more Canadian competitors, and additional trophies were introduced after this time. The Prince of Wales trophy, a solid-silver likeness of a horse, was first donated for presentation to the champion bronc rider in 1923.

Also about this time, the cultural dimension of the fair began to develop more fully. In 1922 Alex Calhoun, Calgary's chief librarian and the first chair of the Calgary Exhibition arts committee, convinced the National Gallery of Canada to send part of its Wembley Exhibition highlighting Canadian painters such as Franklin Carmichael, A.Y. Jackson and Lawren Harris. In 1928 an invitational exhibition by local artists was initiated and immediately became very popular. Art shows have been a part of the Stampede ever since.

The 1923 Stampede was the first to successfully engage the whole city, with motor traffic banned in the mornings to accommodate horse riders, "frontier" fronts put up on businesses, and Calgarians donning "western wear," the forerunner of the iconic white Stetson. Cowtown Calgary was being born during the first Stampede Week, held that year. Eddie King rode his horse through the Club Café dining room, another first, to be repeated by another enthusiastic Calgarian before marvelling

Easterners when the city went to the Grey Cup in Toronto in 1948.

The 1923 Stampede also saw the first chuckwagon races and the first chuckwagon breakfast. Dan Riley, from High River, won the Stetson as the first team owner, and old Bill Somers, a former stage driver from Mosquito Creek, was the winning driver. There was a lot of confusion in organizing the first event, and when whips were used, it turned the race teams into a rebellious bunch of bucking broncs. Whips were banned after that. Chuckwagon races, the long-standing Indian races, novelty chariot races and vaudeville acts were run in the evenings, after this. An Indian Village was set up on the grounds that year. All in all, a pattern was set that year that in many ways survives today.

In 1925 Guy Weadick persuaded his old friend Hoot Gibson to star in a movie titled *The Calgary Stampede*. Edmund Richard Gibson had worked with horses on a ranch when he was a teenager, which led to competition on bucking broncos at California rodeos. "Hoot Owl" Gibson later became much better known as simply Hoot Gibson. He made his first western movie in 1910, the silent *Pride of the Range*, with Tom Mix. Acting was a minor sideline for Gibson, however, and he continued competing in rodeos to make a living. In 1912 he won the all-around championship at the Pendleton Round-Up and the steer roping World Championship at the Calgary Stampede.

The Calgary Stampede film became a great success and carried the name of the Stampede far and wide during the 1920s. Later in the decade, another film was released, *North of 49* (a.k.a. *His Destiny*), financed by Pat Burns, A.E. Cross and John McFarland, and it too reinforced the image of the Stampede.

Indian Commissioner W.M. Graham, fearing bad influence on reserve Indians, placed the Calgary Stampede out of bounds for them in 1925. Only elderly members of the First Nations were able to attend that year. It was also the year that Lord Douglas Haig and Lady Haig attended and

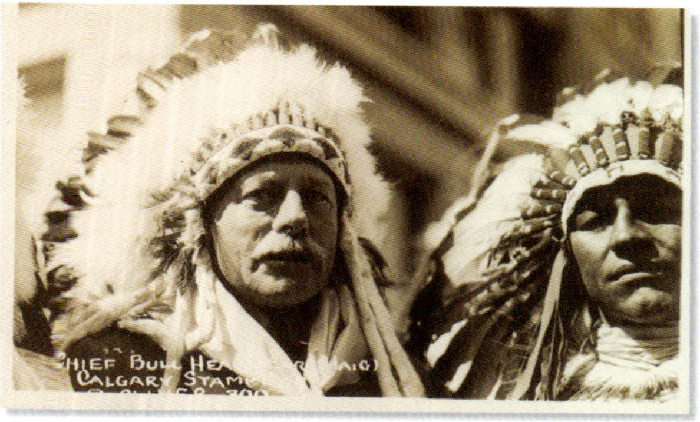

PRAIRIE POSTCARDS PC016482

Lord Haig receiving his honorary Sarcee name, Chief Bull Head.

Haig was made a Sarcee chief. It would not be until the mid-1930s that the Indian Village would once again become a regular and fully supported part of the Stampede.

In 1927 the old "ride 'em into the ground" approach to the bucking contests was replaced by a ten-second time limit, and a new way of grading riding performance was instituted. This was easier on stock – and riders – and allowed the bucking events to end before the evening "entertainment" acts came on.

Attendance increased greatly during the 1920s, putting greater stress on parking space for the increasing number of cars and trucks, as well as stretching all the other service facilities at Victoria Park. In 1928 the Grandstand was expanded, making it the biggest in Canada outside of Toronto's Canadian National Exhibition.

Into the 1930s, as the Great Depression deepened, attendance fell off, and the Exhibition & Stampede suffered a blow on May 3, 1932, when the main exhibits building, built for the 1908 Dominion Exhibition, burned down. A relief force of young single men went to work to get Victoria Park ready for the coming fair, and was able to raise the new Bessborough Building just in time to accommodate that year's exposition. The Exhibition & Stampede became a significant employer for many out-of-work Calgarians for the remainder of the Depression.

Cowboys continued to compete despite Depression austerity that resulted in reduced prize money. A number of stars emerged – men like Herman Linder, Pete Bruisehead, Johnny Lefthand and "The Canada Kid" (from DeWinton, Alberta). By August 1932 it was felt that the Stampede was sufficiently established to terminate the position of Stampede manager, and Richardson ended Guy Weadick's connection with the fair for many years

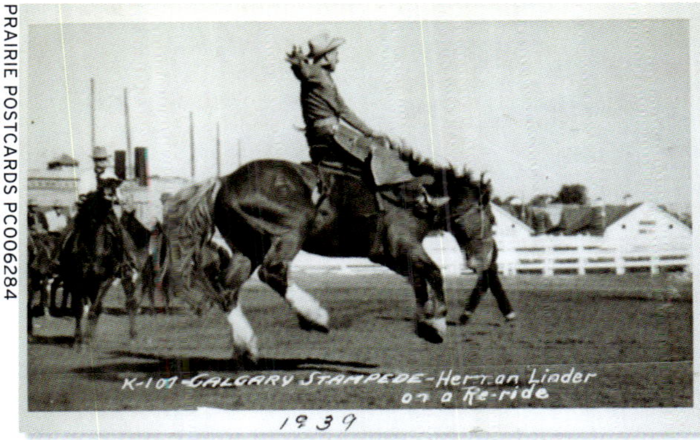

PRAIRIE POSTCARDS PC006284

Herman Linder at the height of his fame. Linder was born in Wisconsin and began riding steers and wild range horses as a boy on his parents' ranch at Cardston, Alberta. In 1921, at a young age, he rode in the Cardston rodeo posing as "Alberta Pearl," a cowgirl. His first competition was also at Cardston, in 1924. At Calgary in 1929, he competed against Pete Knight, Earl Thode, Lee Ferris ("The Canada Kid"), Dan Utley and the Watrin brothers, Leo and Lawrence, and won both the Canadian saddle bronc and the open bareback bronc championships. By the end of 1939, when this postcard was produced by Calgary Photo Supply Co., Linder had won 22 titles in the Calgary Stampede, a record that remains unequalled. He was All-Around champion of Canada seven times, competing in saddle and bareback bronc riding, steer decorating, steer riding and calf roping. He won the North American All-Around five times. In 1934 he won first in bareback, bulls and saddle broncs (Canadian entries) and second in saddle broncs (open entries). The performance earned him North American and Canadian All-Around Cowboy recognition for that season. Linder competed internationally and helped organize the Rodeo Cowboys Association. As a successful rancher, he specialized in Maine-Anjou beef cattle and won many awards. Herman and Agnes Linder received the Alberta Master Farm Family Award in 1971.

PRAIRIE POSTCARDS PC006205

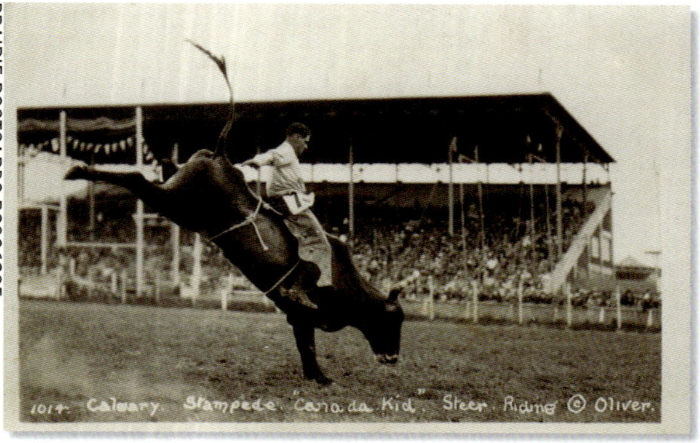

Lee Ferris, "The Canada Kid," steer riding at Calgary. Ferris was born at his grandmother's home in North Dakota in 1908, and immigrated with his family to Swan Valley, Alberta, in 1913. In 1924 he began his rodeo career at the age of sixteen. At that time, there were very few rodeo contestants from Canada who rode in the United States, so it wasn't long before Ferris earned the title "The Canada Kid."
At the 1929 Calgary Stampede, Ferris was injured quite seriously while riding a longhorn steer when a horn gouged his right eye. The Canada Kid finished his ride and won first money for the day but never regained sight in his injured eye. Ferris was Canadian All-Around Champion 1928 and 1929, Steer Riding Champion 1928 and Bareback Riding Champion 1930 and 1931 at the Calgary Stampede. He died in 1943. W.J. Oliver is credited with this historic image of the great early Stampede rider.

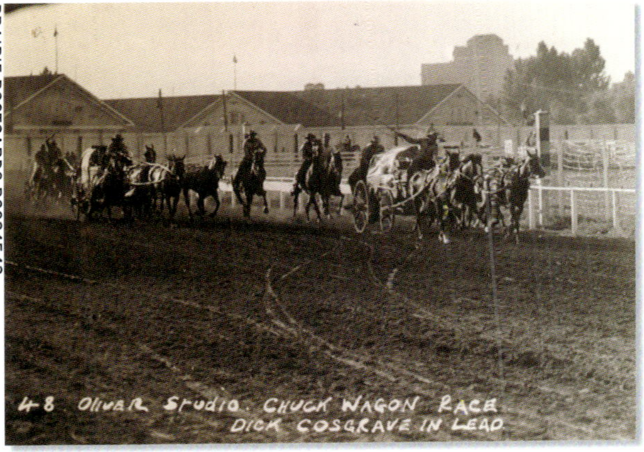

PRAIRIE POSTCARDS PC024542

This great W.J. Oliver image is of Dick Cosgrave leading the field with his chuckwagon team. Cosgrave, from Rosebud, Alberta, was a ten-time winner of the event.

to come. Weadick left the Stampede an embittered man who felt that his original vision had been lost in recent years through the parsimonious restraints of the board.

A.E. Cross, one of the Big Four, died in 1932. His role on the board, and later as chairman, was assumed later by his son James, a regular chuckwagon race outrider since 1923. After 1933, under Jim Cross's influence, cash prizes were instituted for the chuckwagon races, and the contests became a more prominent part of the annual event. In 1936 entrants were required to wear colourful regalia, and all chuckwagon teams and wagons had to adopt distinctive colours. Dick Cosgrave and Clem Gardner would dominate the sport for some time after 1933.

Jack Dillon organized the Alberta Stampede Directors Association in 1933, to provide a common round table for directors from across the province. Following the success of the early Calgary events, many Alberta communities had kicked off their own local ones, and soon there were little stampedes carrying on throughout the province and forming a sort of bush league to support aspiring big-time competitors. During the Depression many cowboys, sometimes lacking even their entry fees, also needed to work at odd jobs between the official contests. During Stampede Week, cowboys could earn $3.50 daily even for unskilled labour, and up to $8 a day working as a pickup man, or backup rider, whose job was to help a bronc rider dismount safely at the end of his event. During the Depression this money was a real help to the men who were expected to staff the events.

Historical pageantry was one of the principal inspirations for the first Calgary celebrations, and in 1934 this tradition continued through events

PRAIRIE POSTCARDS PC012020

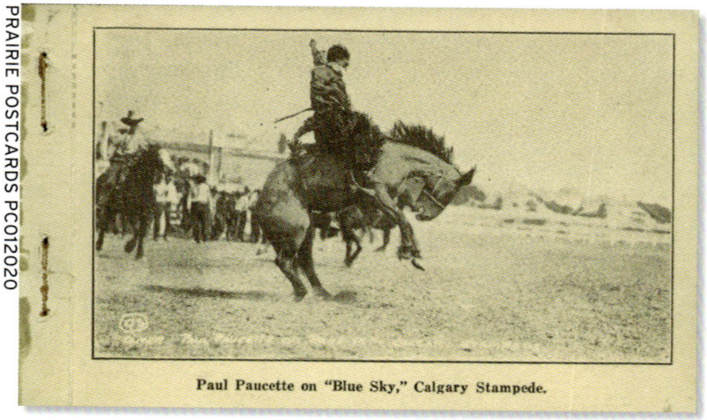

Paul Paucette on Blue Sky in the finals at the Calgary Stampede, from a booklet of ten postcards, many with images by W.J. Oliver, distributed by Max Zack of Calgary.

PRAIRIE POSTCARDS PC006160

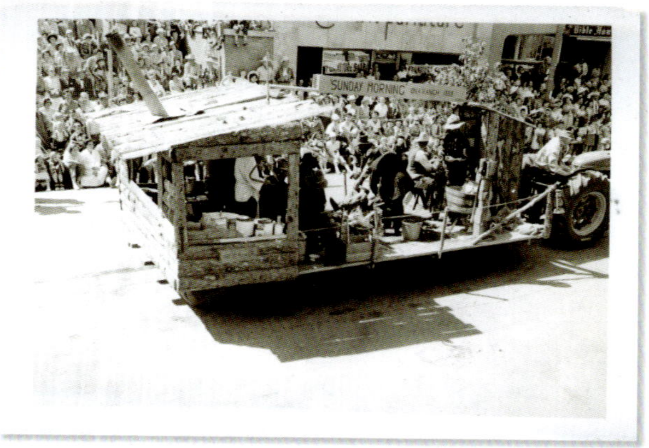

Parade pageantry often tipped the hat to the early ranching heritage of southern Alberta. "Sunday morning on the ranch, 1888" was a float that clearly showed this romantic view.

like the golden anniversary of the town of Calgary, celebrated in that year's parade by including pioneers like Colonel James Walker, an original founder of the Calgary fair in 1884. Prime Minister R.B. Bennett returned to the city to officiate at the opening of the big event. The arrival of the North-West Mounted Police at Fort Calgary in 1875 was celebrated in 1935 with bigger and better pageants.

Many of the old guard began to disappear during the 1930s and '40s. Besides A.E. Cross in 1932, Colonel Walker and Pat Burns passed away in 1936 and Colonel Wolley-Dod in 1937.

The legendary Pete Knight also died in 1937. He had won bronc championships at Calgary in 1927, 1930, 1932 and 1933. Knight took his first World Championship in 1926 and repeated the feat in 1932, 1933, 1935 and 1936. Knight was the top contender again in 1937, but he

PRAIRIE POSTCARDS PC024555A

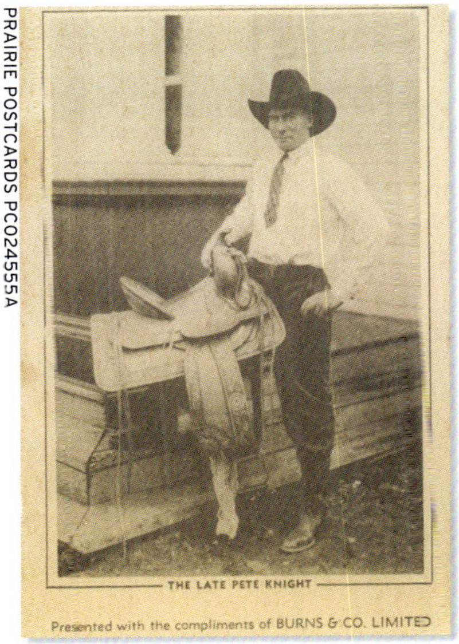

PRAIRIE POSTCARDS PC024555B

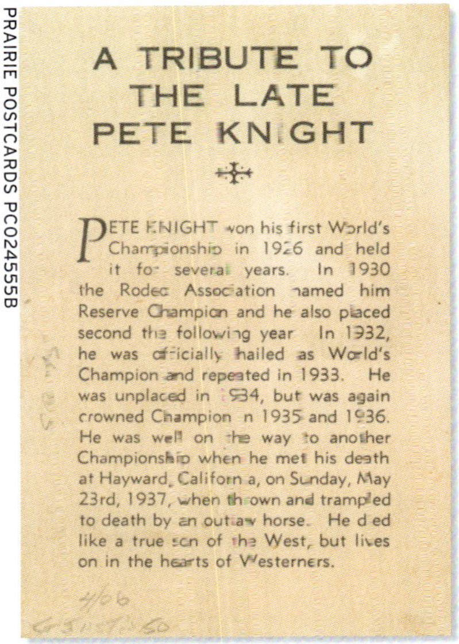

A TRIBUTE TO THE LATE PETE KNIGHT

PETE KNIGHT won his first World's Championship in 1926 and held it for several years. In 1930 the Rodeo Association named him Reserve Champion and he also placed second the following year. In 1932, he was officially hailed as World's Champion and repeated in 1933. He was unplaced in 1934, but was again crowned Champion in 1935 and 1936. He was well on the way to another Championship when he met his death at Hayward, California, on Sunday, May 23rd, 1937, when thrown and trampled to death by an outlaw horse. He died like a true son of the West, but lives on in the hearts of Westerners.

The passing of Pete Knight, a "true son of the West" and a Stampede hero, was commemorated in a brochure published by Burns & Company in 1937.

was thrown and trampled to death by a bucking horse on May 23. A published tribute said that Knight "died like a true son of the West, but lives on in the hearts of Westerners."

Another of the old guard to disappear from the Stampede scene was Ernie Richardson, who retired in 1940. By then the Second World War had begun.

While the Edmonton Exhibition was suspended during the war, the Calgary Exhibition & Stampede fared better with an upsurge in the southern Alberta

PRAIRIE POSTCARDS PC010153

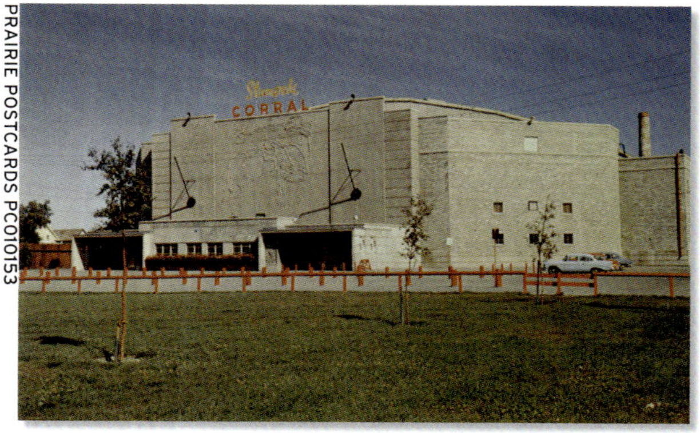

Over the years, the Stampede Corral has also been known as the Calgary Corral and The Corral at Stampede Park. Grant-Mann Lithographers Ltd. published this view, distributed by Alberta News Ltd., shortly after the new Corral opened on December 15, 1950, replacing the old Victoria Arena. Seating nearly 6,500, the building was the largest arena in Canada west of Toronto at that time. Originally built to house hockey, the Corral has also hosted Davis Cup tennis as well as the famous rodeo, plus such historic events as the 1972 World Figure Skating Championships and 1988 Winter Olympics figure skating and hockey. For years, the Corral was also home to the great old wrestling supershows promoted by Stu Hart's Stampede Wrestling, especially during Stampede Week.

livestock industry. The purebred bull shows reflected this change, attracting many entrants with its prizes, and buoying the entire organization, despite the fact that the RCAF and the Canadian Army occupied buildings on the grounds. In 1944 a special wartime federal permit was obtained to allow a large extension to the livestock pavilion, bringing the number of stalls to a thousand, to accommodate the increased numbers of purebred bull entrants. Gasoline rationing and the disappearance of star American attractions after the United States entered the war in 1942 added to the problems. However, the rodeo events more than compensated for cutbacks in areas like the midway shows.

Between 1945 and 1950 the spirit of postwar reconstruction extended to rebuilding the Exhibition & Stampede grounds. The rise of the Calgary Stampeders football team, culminating in their Grey Cup triumph in Toronto in 1948, fuelled the renewed enthusiasm that sustained grand plans for the Stampede. When the Stampede Corral building opened in 1950, it ushered in the postwar Stampede in a big way, despite the terrible weather of that July. In 1951 a special October Stampede event held for the first visit of Princess Elizabeth and Prince Philip was marred by a blizzard.

The 1950s would see increasingly successful Stampedes. After the discovery of oil at Leduc, Alberta, in 1947 launched an era of prosperity, the province began to really build on the wartime boom. Many Americans who followed the oil companies north to Calgary and Edmonton were already familiar with rodeos, and attendance continued to increase. Marty Wood, the first native Calgarian to win the North American Saddle championship, in 1955, drove the local excitement that year. Slim Pickens often worked the Stampede as a rodeo clown. Duncan Renaldo and Leo Carillo (the Cisco Kid and Pancho) returned several times during their years of television fame to participate in the parades and visit hospitalized Calgary children. They were such a hit that it encouraged the Stampede to bring other personalities in, though with mixed success.

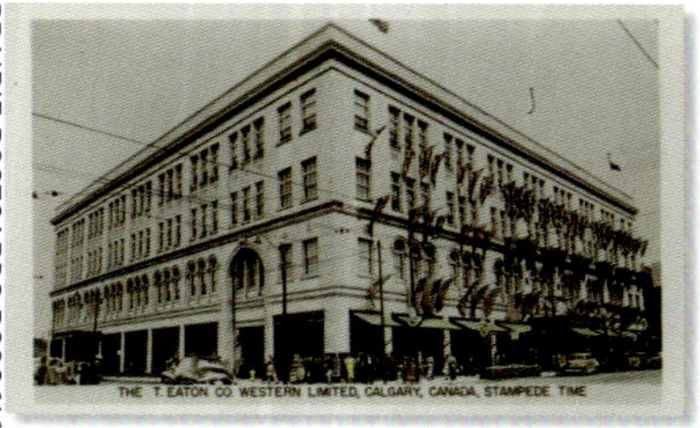

PRAIRIE POSTCARDS PC006162

Downtown Calgary came alive with decorations during Stampede Week. Here, the T. Eaton Co. store at 8th Avenue and 4th Street SW unfurls Union Jacks and Old Glory to welcome cowboys from across the North American West. Gowen Sutton Co. of Vancouver published this card.

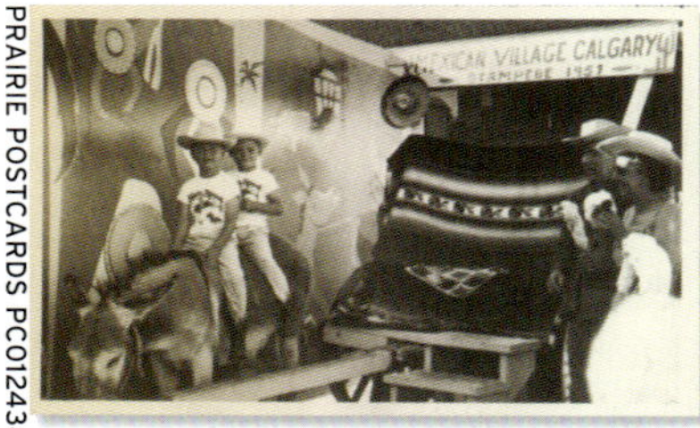

PRAIRIE POSTCARDS PC0124344

The 1957 Mexican Village provided the kind of "value added" attractions that Stampede visitors had come to expect.

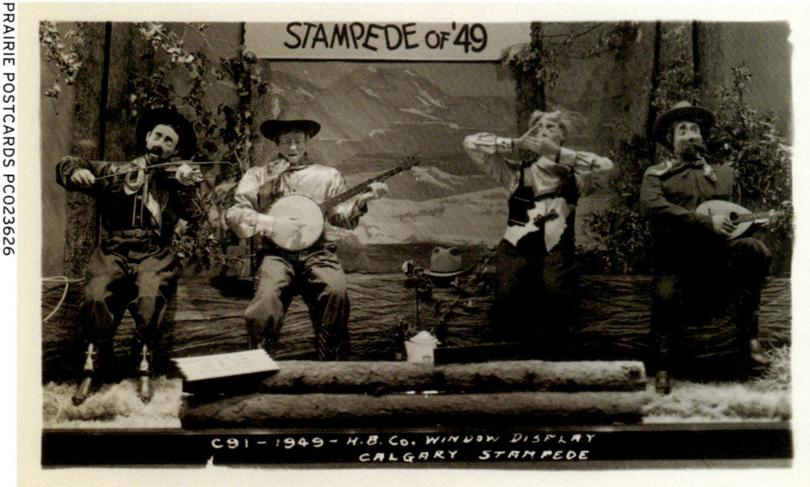

PRAIRIE POSTCARDS PC023626

This 1949 window display in the Hudson's Bay Co. department store was typical during Stampede Week.

The Stampede grounds developed significantly during the 1950s. Besides the Stampede Corral in 1950, a new parimutuel facility was built in 1951. In 1954 City structures like the old bus barns were removed to make room for 15 additional acres between the east boundary and the Elbow River, expanding Stampede Park to 114 acres. The racetrack was rebuilt that same year, and in 1959 the Big Four Building, including a curling rink, was completed. It was at this time also that the Bessborough Building was moved to the vicinity of the race barn and converted into race horse winter quarters. The Willingdon Building, where for years Stampede attendees had found accommodation, was also moved, to the Sunshine Auto Camp grounds, and turned into a storage warehouse.

The 1959 Stampede was very successful. That year, Queen Elizabeth and Prince Philip attended for the second time, and US crooner Bing Crosby was the honorary parade marshal. In 1960 free outdoor entertainment became a regular feature of the Stampede, in order to mollify patrons who were enraged by the doubling of the entrance fee to fifty cents. Prime Minister John Diefenbaker officially opened the events, while Bing Crosby returned with Phil Harris and Alice Faye. Harris was the parade marshal that year. Roy Rogers came to the show in 1962, followed as parade marshal by Bob Hope, Walt Disney, Robert Kennedy, Gordie Howe, Nancy Green, Earl Mountbatten of Burma

PRAIRIE POSTCARDS PC010168

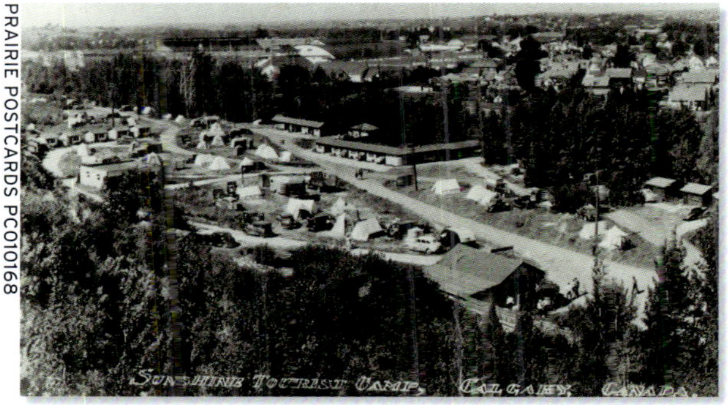

Over several decades, Stampede patrons would stay at the Sunshine Auto Camp, just outside the grounds. This early view was taken during Stampede Week.

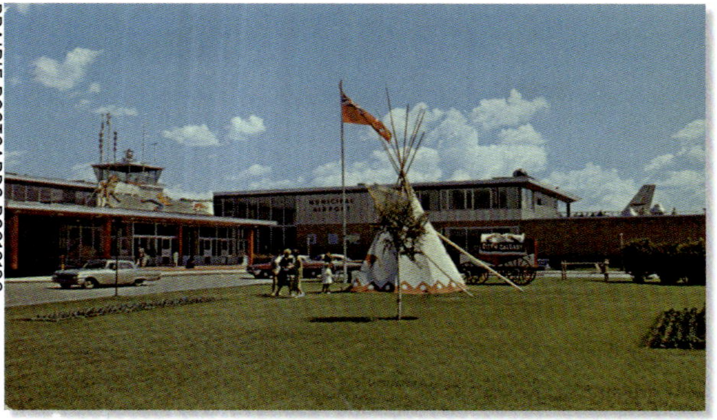

PRAIRIE POSTCARDS PC010138

This circa 1971 view of Calgary Municipal Airport, distributed by United News (Wholesalers) Ltd. of Calgary, features representations of the city's heritage. Text on the reverse of the card reads in part: "The chuckwagon shown in the picture outside the terminal building is symbolic of Calgary's world-famous annual Stampede."

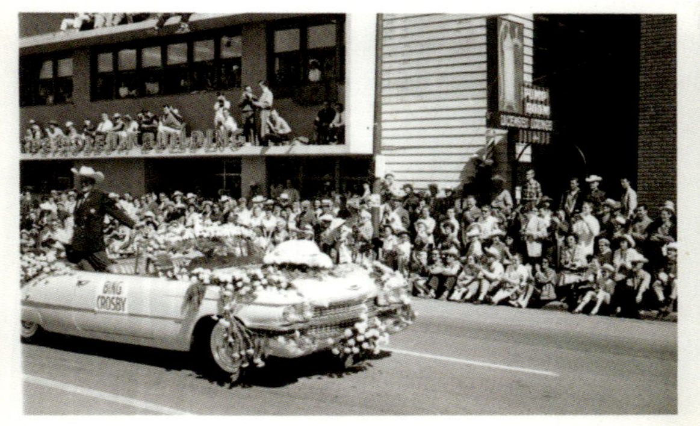

PRAIRIE POSTCARDS PC006159

Bing Crosby, Calgary Stampede parade marshal 1959.

and the Duke and Duchess of Kent.

Stampede spirit – and spirits – are remembered by many for Mayor Harry Hays's annual Stampede breakfasts in the early 1960s, during which he served up his infamous alcoholic "syllabub" from a bathtub to dignitaries from far and wide.

In 1968 Calgary City Council approved yet another Stampede Park expansion, northward to 14th Avenue SE, which required the removal of some older homes. New grandstand and horse racing facilities were completed in 1974. The Exhibition Grounds was renamed Stampede Park in 1975, the centennial of the founding of Fort Calgary. The Roundup Centre would follow in time. As the Stampede expanded and became more urbanized and less agricultural and "Western," it would change in many ways. But the old dream of cowboys, bucking broncs and parade pageantry remains a big part of the Stampede story a hundred years on.

The vintage postcards in this collection represent some of the finest images captured by several famous professional photographers as well as many

PRAIRIE POSTCARDS PC012157

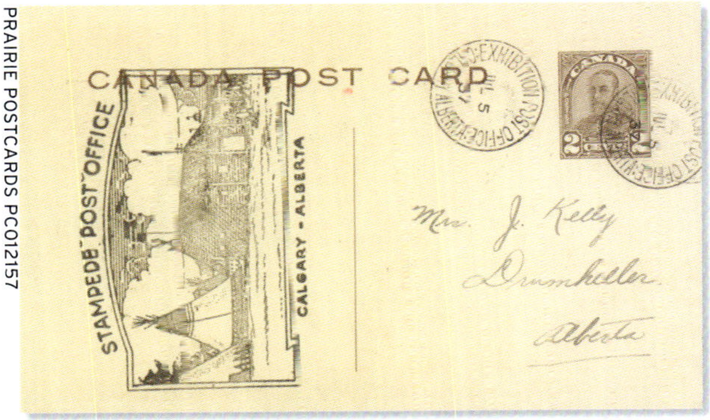

This decorative stamp identifies the Calgary Stampede post office, on the grounds from which so many thousands of postcards were mailed over the years.

PRAIRIE POSTCARDS PC015629

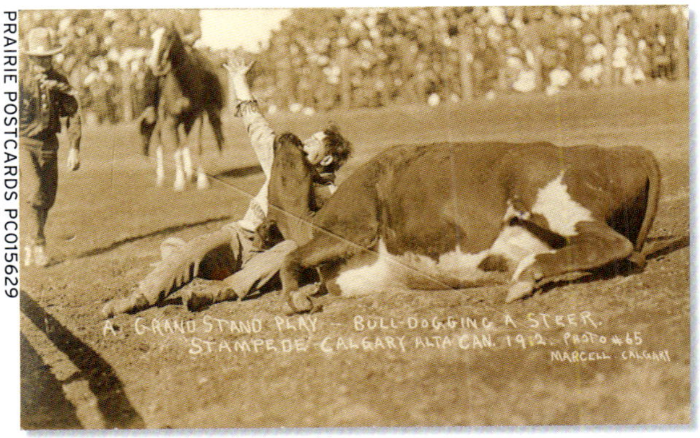

Marcell of Calgary, the first official Stampede photographer, captured this great "grandstand play" at the 1912 Stampede.

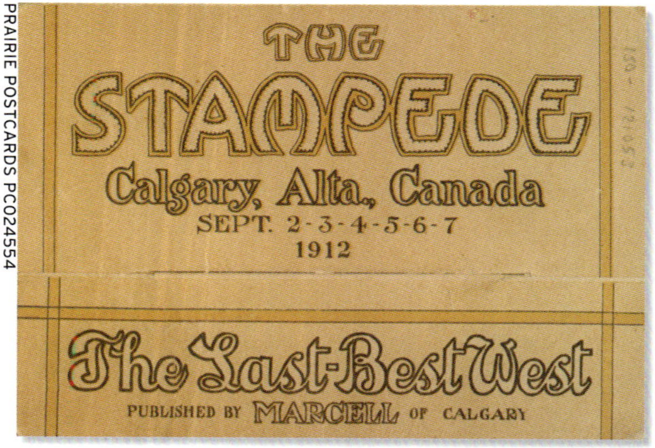

PRAIRIE POSTCARDS PC024554

Marcell of Calgary published a collection of images from the first Stampede under this cover in 1912.

talented amateurs. Many of these images, such as "Grandstand Play," have attained the status of cultural icons, reminding us of the great early days of the Stampede.

Marcus Belmont Marcell (1869–1939) was born Milward Belmont Davis in Louisville, Kentucky, where his father worked as a photographer. He left home in 1888, making his living as an itinerant photographer, and later worked for William Randolph Hearst's *New York Journal.* Davis changed his name to Marcus Belmont Marcell, and in 1910 settled in Portland, Oregon, where he set up a portrait studio. From 1911 through 1914 Marcell travelled across the western United States and Canada, following the emerging rodeo circuit as a photographer and meeting men like Guy Weadick. He moved to Calgary in 1912 at the invitation of Weadick, who arranged for him to become the official photographer of the first Calgary Stampede. From 1912 to 1914, Marcell operated two portrait studios in Calgary and produced at least two hundred views of the Stampede. The Calgary *News-Telegram* reported that he also produced a feature-length film of the 1912 events, shown at the Empress Theatre that September. Marcell photographed the Winnipeg Stampede in 1913, and soon moved to Miles City, Montana, where he opened another portrait studio.

R.R. Doubleday was one of the greatest photographers to work the early Stampedes and capture their atmosphere for later generations. He had been introduced to the public by the famous US humorist Will Rogers, who wrote in his newspaper column in 1926 that Doubleday "is the one that has taken 90 per cent of the good rodeo pictures ever made." Many consider him to be the first rodeo photographer of note. Doubleday exploited the popular photographic-postcard genre and had such success at it that he came to be known as the Rodeo Postcard King. Likely born Edward Cochran in Canton, Ohio, on July 4, 1881, he later changed his name to Ralph Russell Doubleday and took up rodeo photography seriously about 1910 after a successful stint at the Cheyenne (Wyoming) Frontier Days. For years he promoted the Miller Brothers 101 Ranch Wild West show. "Old Dub" was the show's official arena photographer, working across the West at rodeos large and small at Calgary, Pendleton, Cheyenne, Belle Fourche, Fort Worth, Casper, Deadwood and San Antonio. Doubleday's career coincided with the craze for photographic postcards during the first decades of the 20th century, and with an estimated 30 million sold, it made him a wealthy man. He died in 1958 and was posthumously inducted into the Rodeo Historical Society's Rodeo Hall of Fame in 1988.

W.J. Oliver (1887–1954) was another of the early photographers who worked the Stampedes for material. Born in England, William John Oliver became interested in photography after winning a camera in a contest. He immigrated to southern Alberta in 1910, first serving as a camera assistant at the Frederick B. Cooper Photographic Studio in Calgary, then working for the *Morning Albertan* newspaper. In 1912 he opened the W.J. Oliver Photographic Studio and joined the *Calgary Herald* as a staff photographer. Throughout the 1920s and 1930s Oliver took many photos of the Calgary Stampede, and travelled across Canada making stills and films for the National Parks

Branch, Fox Movietone News and other clients. In 1942 he sold his studio to devote more time to his Diamond L ranch, near Millarville, Alberta.

Calgarian Joe Rosettis held his own with the best of the rodeo photographers, and created an impressive body of work over the years. The Rosettis Studio produced many of the strong images that presented the Stampede to an international public. Joseph L. Rosettis (1909–1965) was born in Glasgow to a Lithuanian family that then immigrated to Toronto when Joe was still an infant. Rosettis would work all across the country, for clients such as Associated Screen News of Montreal, for which he also travelled internationally. He did promotional photography for the CPR and later worked as a staff photographer at the *Calgary Herald*. Joe married Kay in 1940 and the couple moved to Calgary. In 1943 they opened their own studio and in 1952 moved the studio to their home, where Kay often worked in the darkroom. Rosettis Studio produced a series of great photographic images of the Calgary Stampede between 1944 and 1965.

In addition to the photographers listed, other individuals as well as local, regional and national publishers distributed a vast array of postcards over the years. Many of these are included in this book. I hope that readers will enjoy them as much as I did during the research.

THE POSTCARDS

PRAIRIE POSTCARDS PC006152

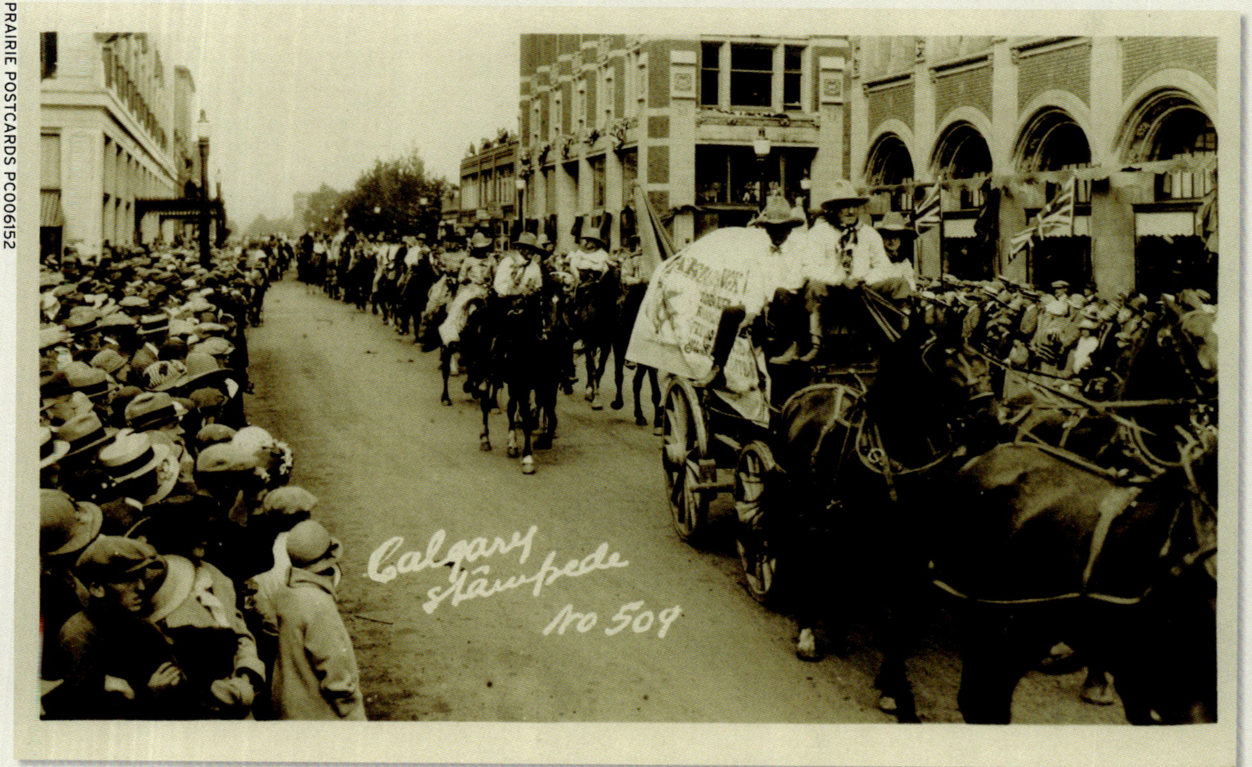

The Calgary Stampede parade during the 1920s. Published by McDermid Photo Laboratories of Calgary.

PRAIRIE POSTCARDS PC006138

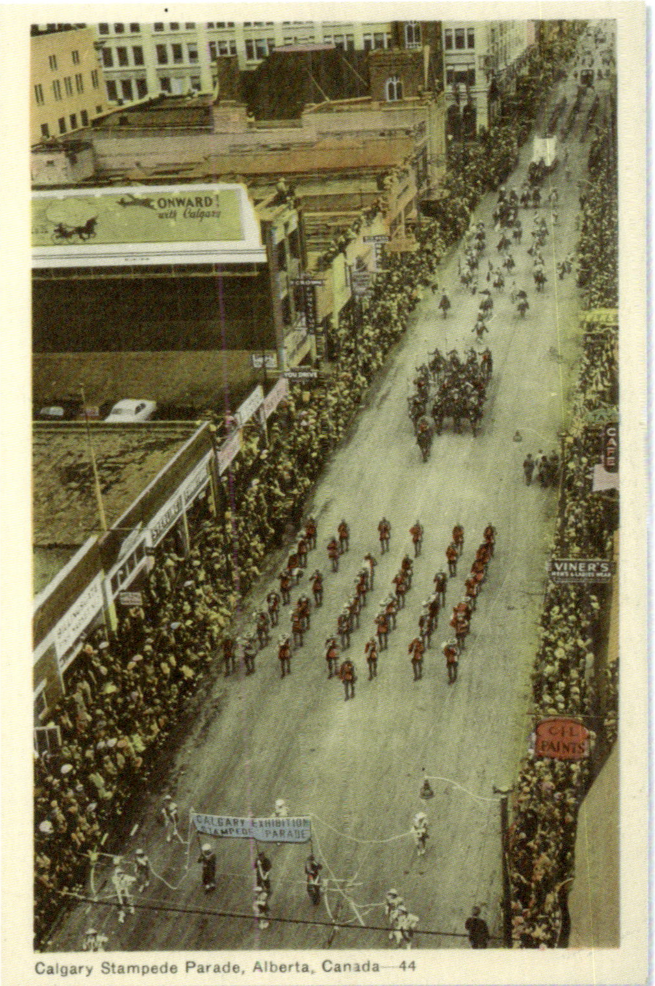

This tinted bird's-eye view of the Calgary Stampede parade in the early 1950s includes a contingent of Royal Canadian Mounted Police.

PC016462

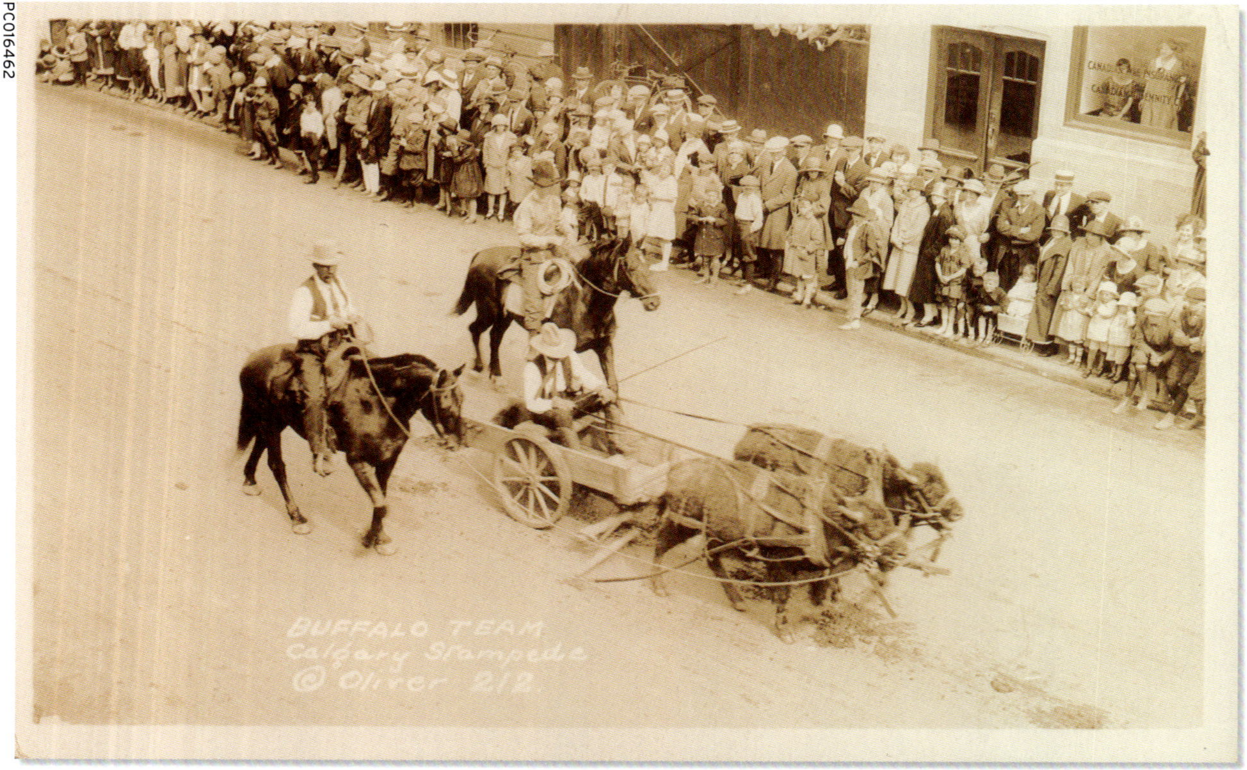

Buffalo team

PRAIRIE POSTCARDS PC006004

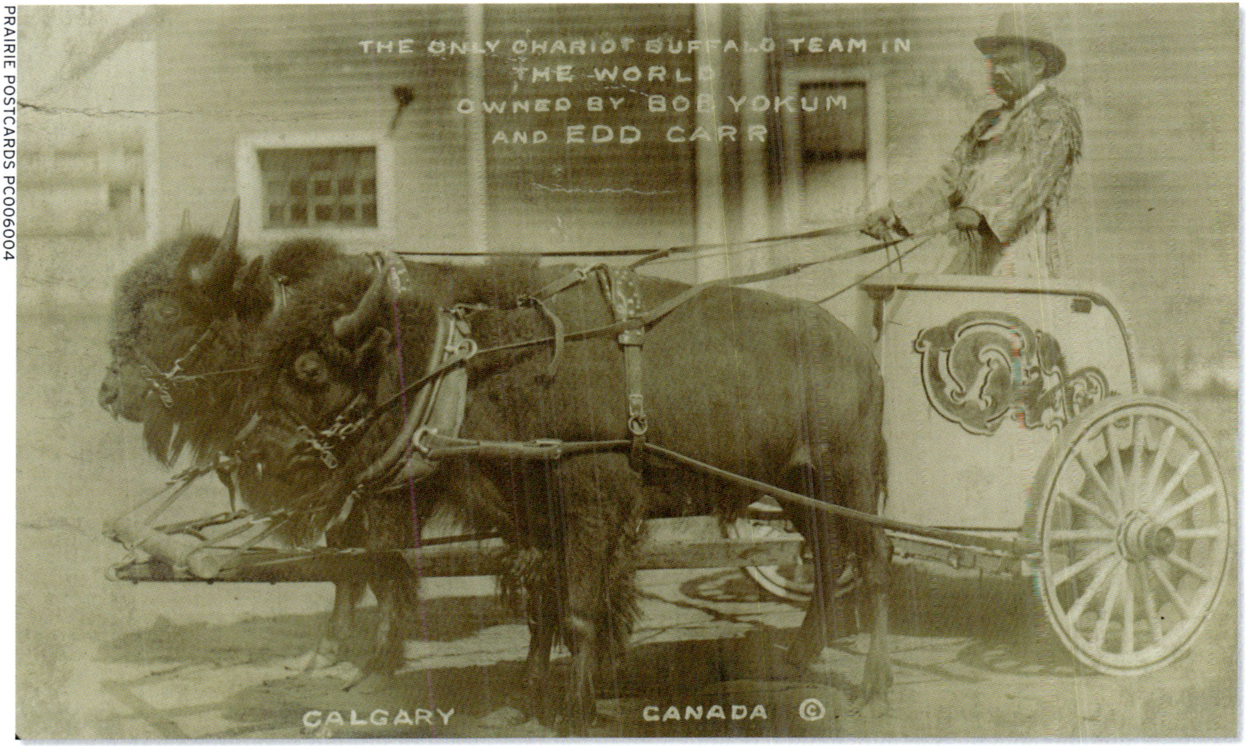

Bob Yokum and Edd Carr, from South Dakota, brought "the only chariot buffalo team in the world" to the first Calgary Exhibition & Stampede in 1912.

PRAIRIE POSTCARDS PC006148

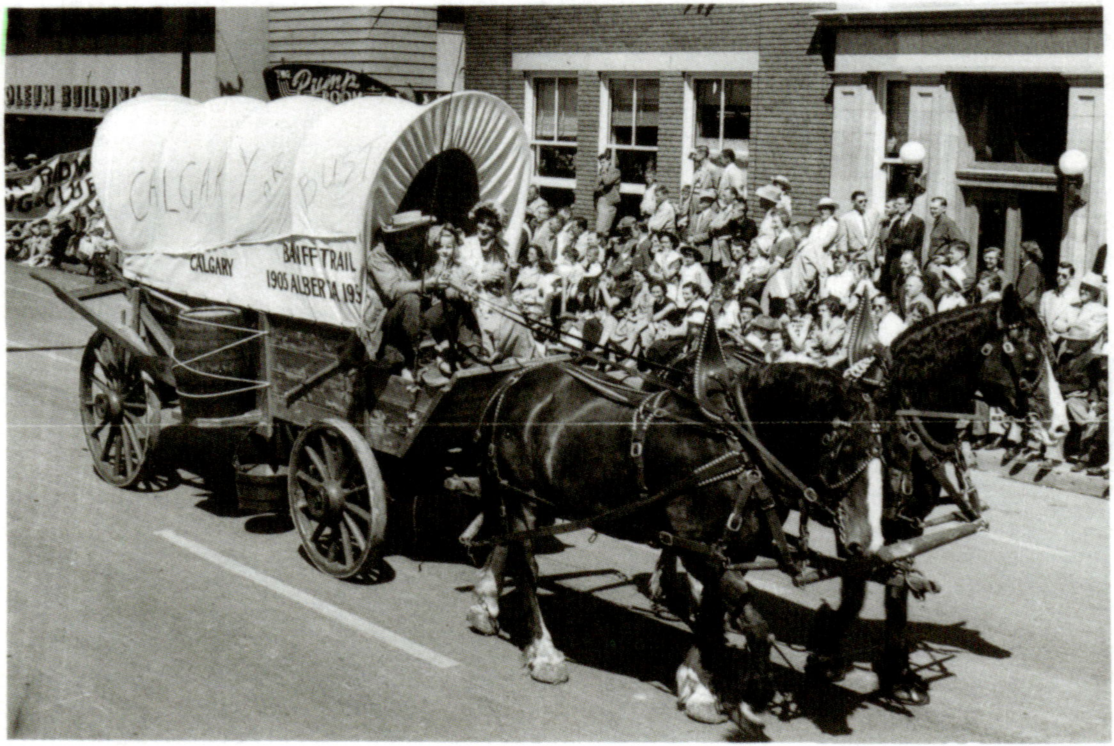

"Calgary or Bust," a covered wagon in the Alberta Golden Jubilee Stampede parade in 1955.

PRAIRIE POSTCARDS PC006142

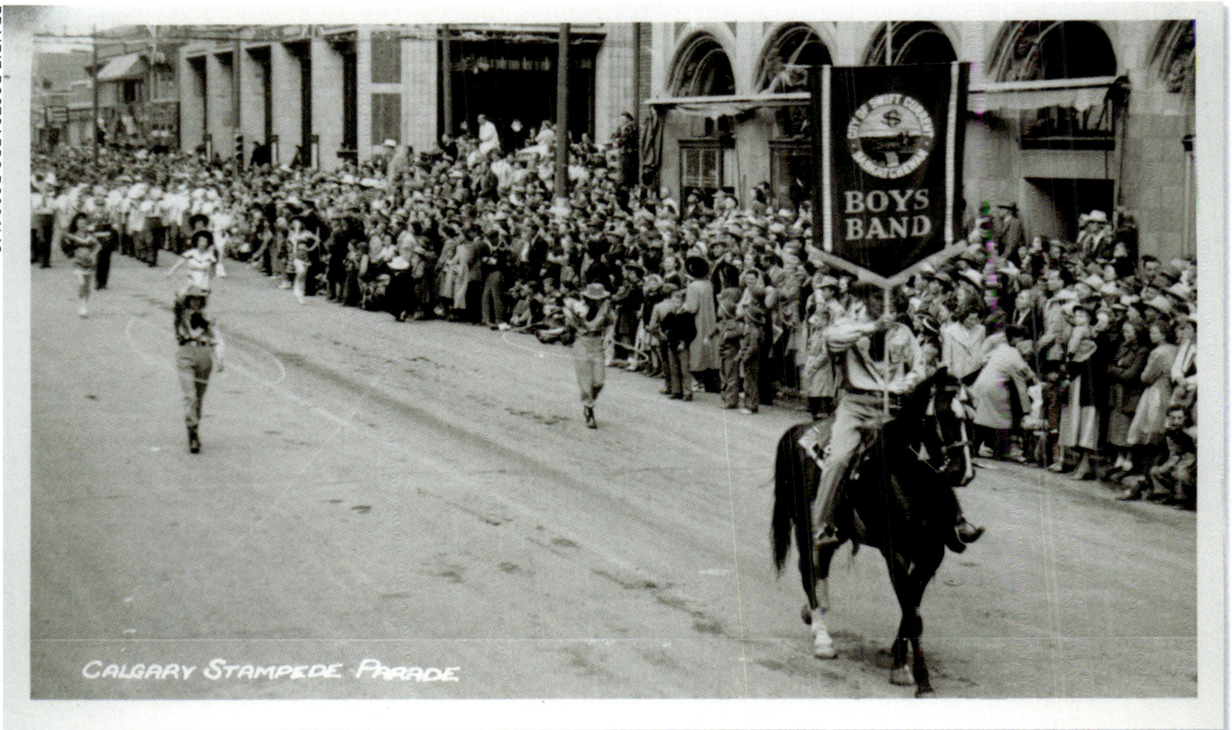

The Calgary Stampede parade in 1950.

PRAIRIE POSTCARDS PC006149

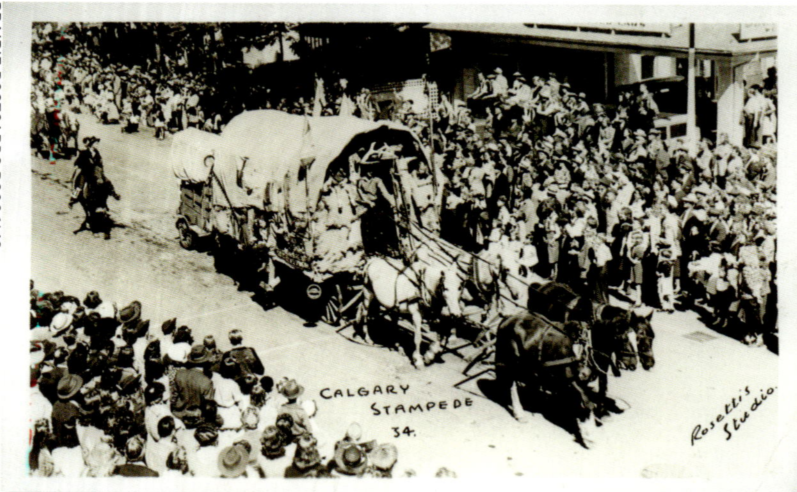

Another great Rosettis postcard of the momentous 1948 Stampede parade. The Rosettis Studio produced many of the strong images that presented the Stampede to an international public, creating an impressive body of work over the years.

PRAIRIE POSTCARDS PC006143

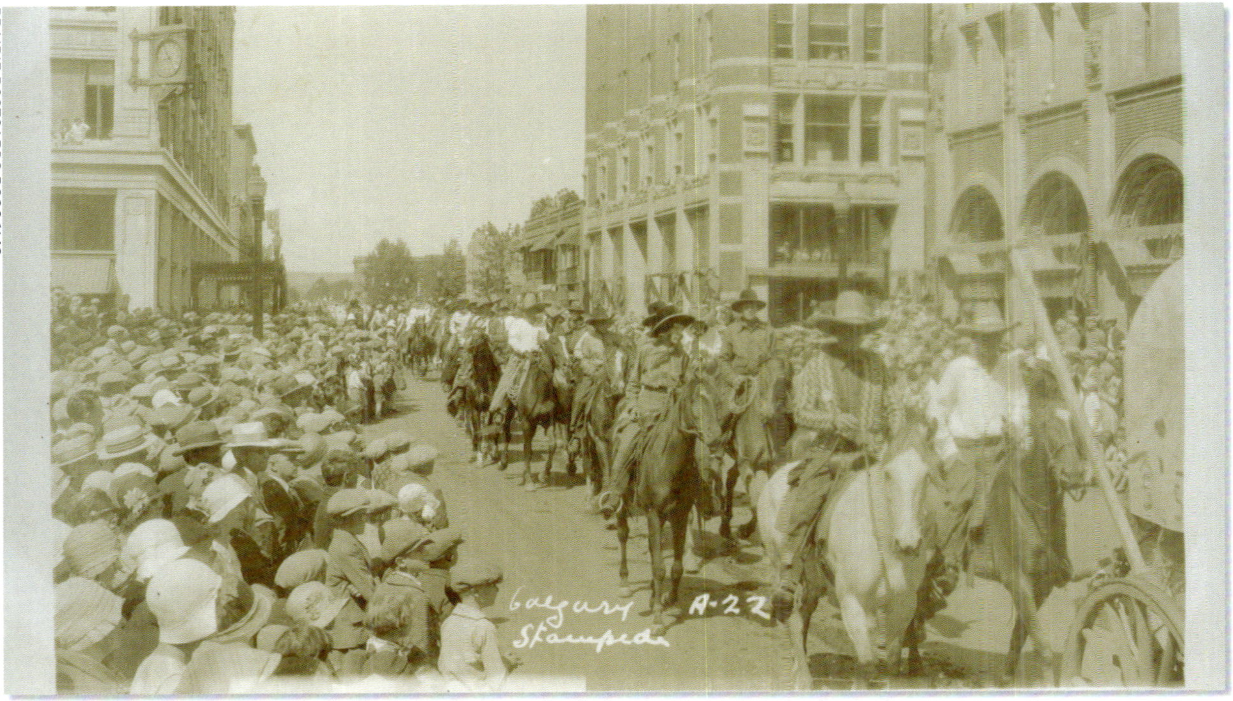

Fashions in hats changed over the years, for cowboys as well as spectators. This view, taken by McDermid Photo Laboratories of Calgary in about 1925, demonstrates this through a glimpse of the moment when the competing cowboys rode by.

PRAIRIE POSTCARDS PC006154

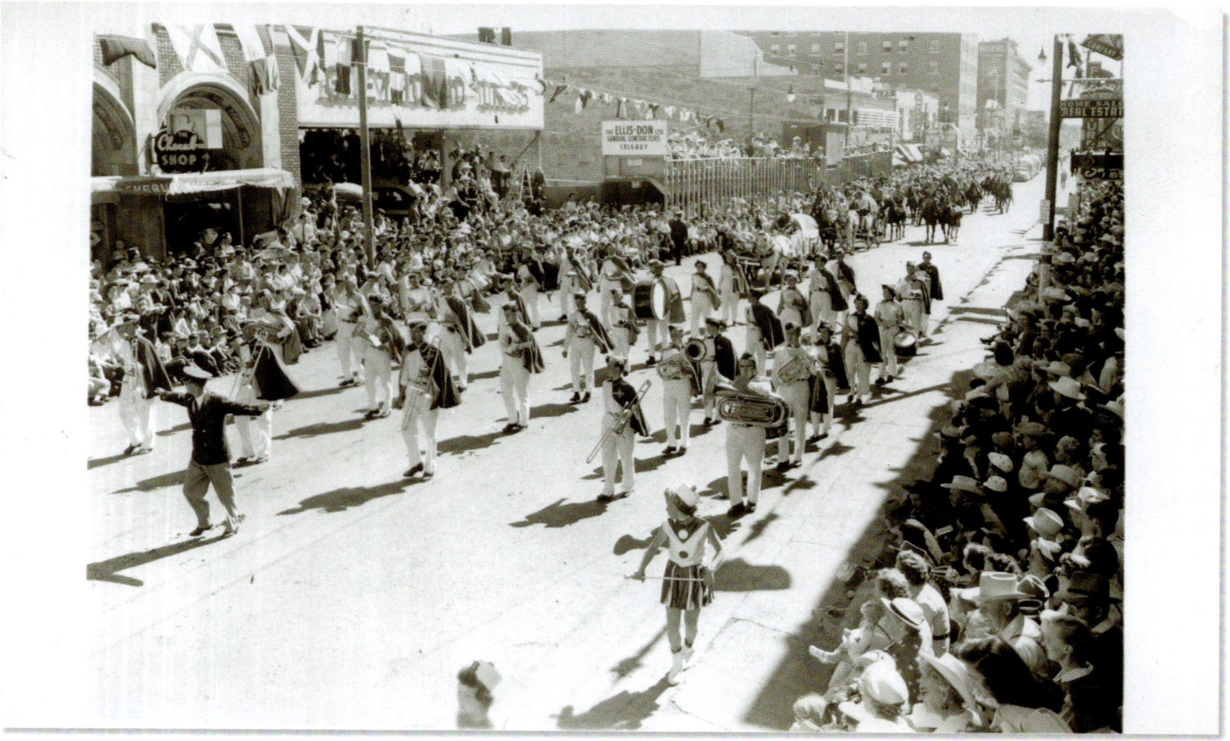

Marching bands became a bigger part of the Calgary Stampede parades during the 1950s. This postcard was produced about 1956.

PRAIRIE POSTCARDS PC006156

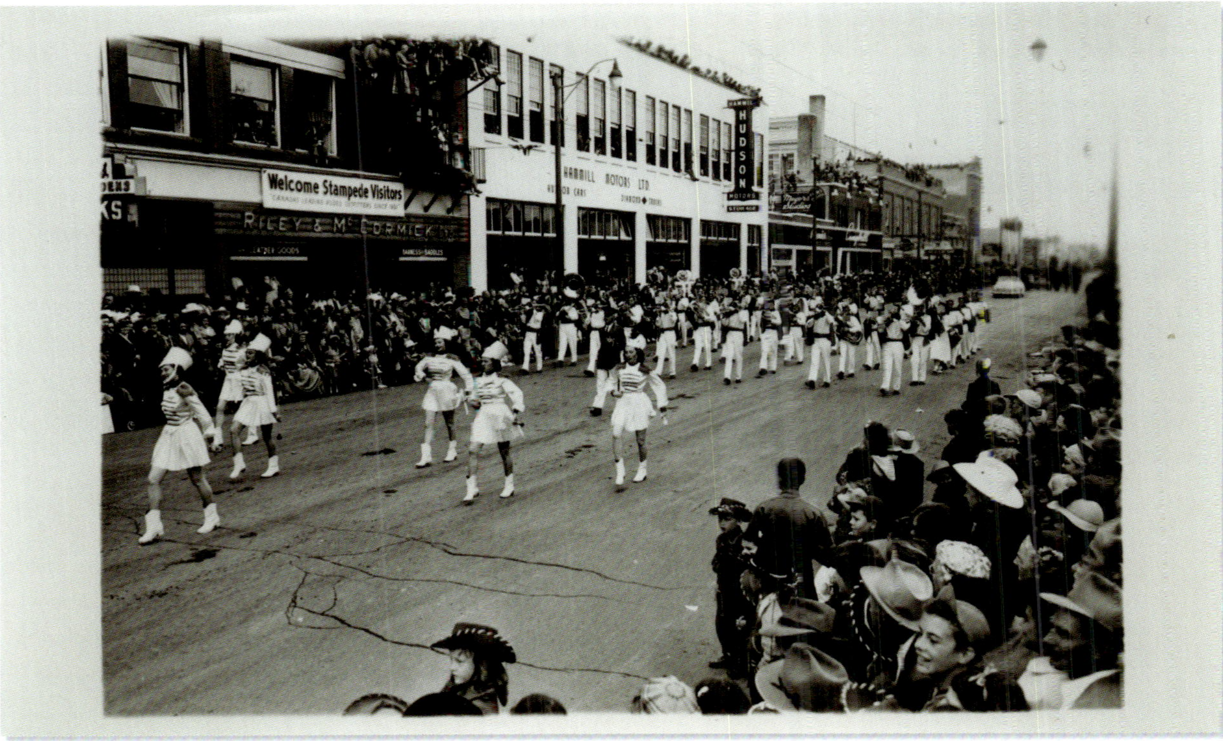

The marching band from Taber, Alberta, was a regular participant in the Calgary Stampede parades of the 1950s.

PRAIRIE POSTCARDS PC012028

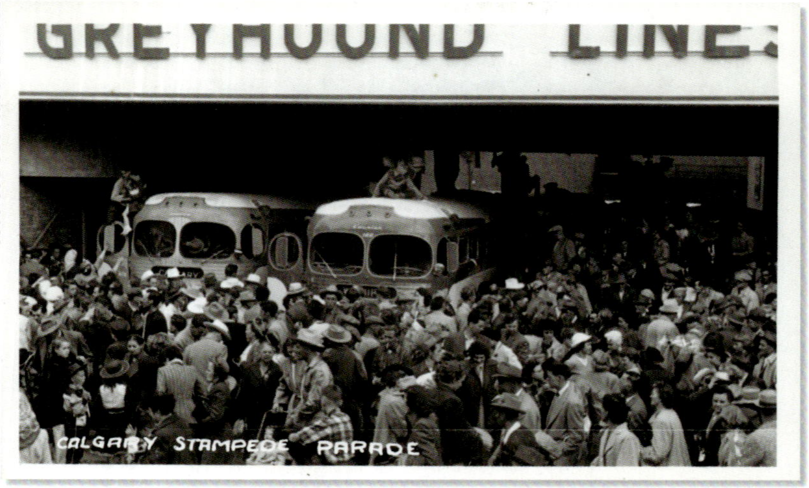

The Calgary Stampede reached another crescendo of enthusiasm in 1948, when the Stampeders football team went east to vie for the 36th Grey Cup. They went on to defeat the Ottawa Rough Riders 12–7 at Toronto's Varsity Stadium on November 27. McDermid Drug Co. published this image of the crowd thronging the Calgary Greyhound bus station that year. Calgarians visiting Toronto for the game famously upheld a celebrated early Stampede tradition by riding horses into the lobby of the upscale Royal York Hotel downtown, and wowed the easterners with pancake breakfasts on the steps of City Hall.

PRAIRIE POSTCARDS PC006302

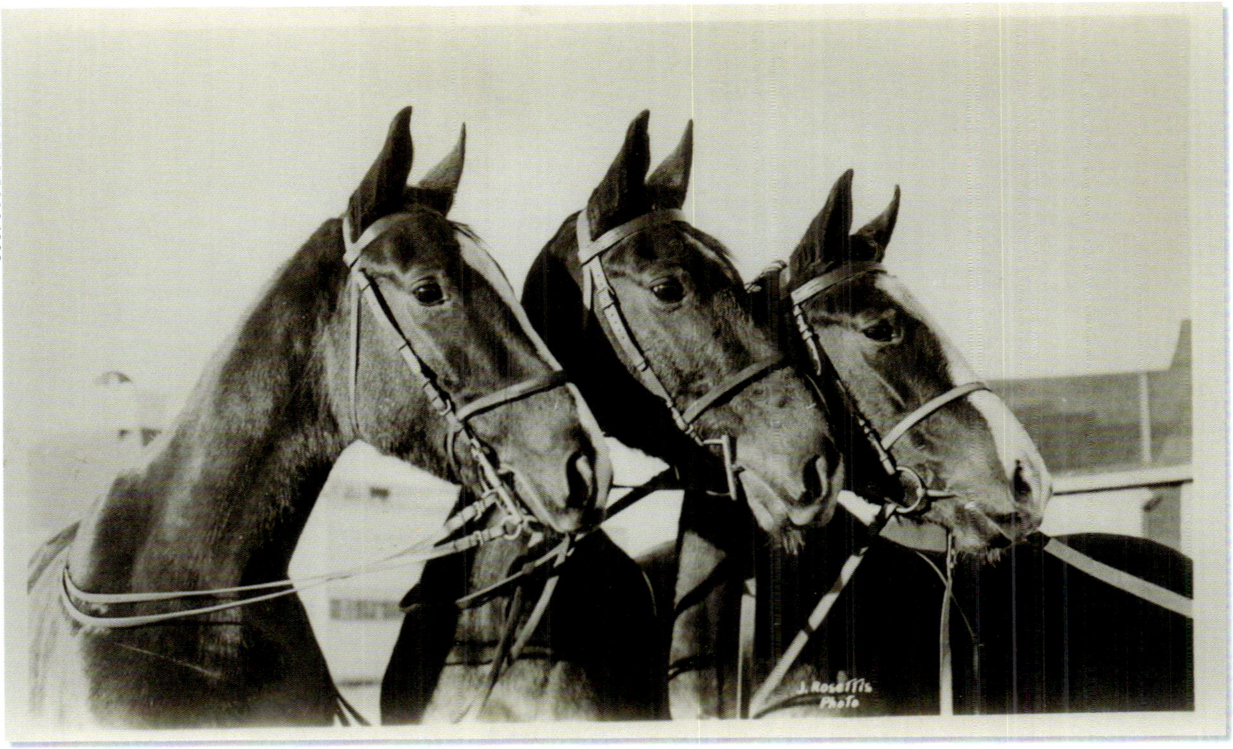

This marvellous portrait of three horses at the Calgary Stampede is a tribute to the Rosettis Studio and the role of these high-spirited equine competitors, without which there would never have been a Stampede.

PRAIRIE POSTCARDS PC006158

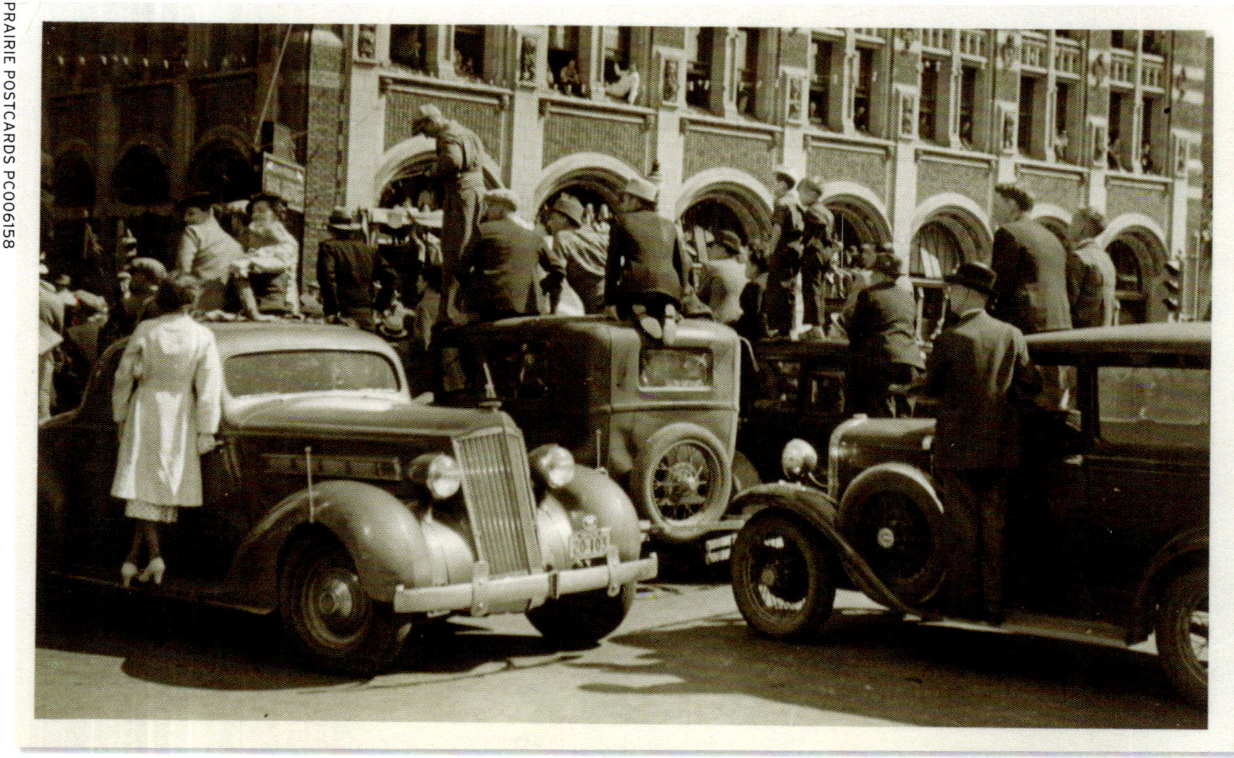

People crowd the route for the 1937 Stampede parade, craning their necks to see the passing show.

PC024563

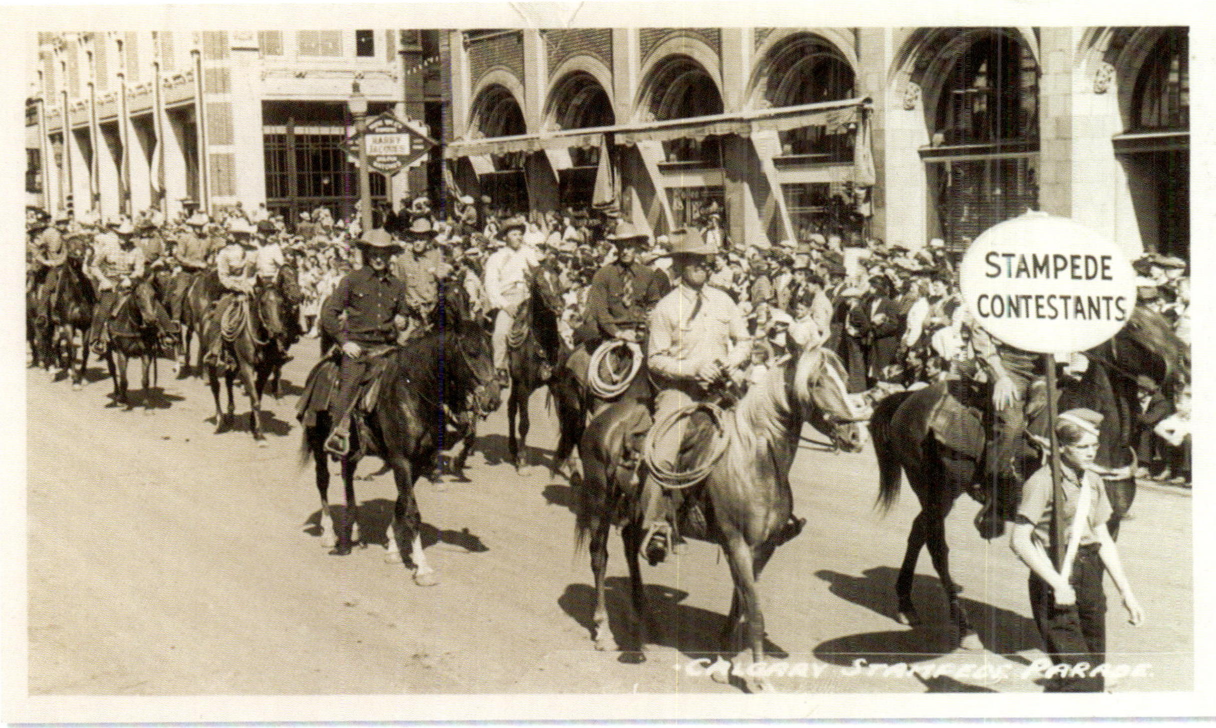

Stampede competition riders

PRAIRIE POSTCARDS PC012022

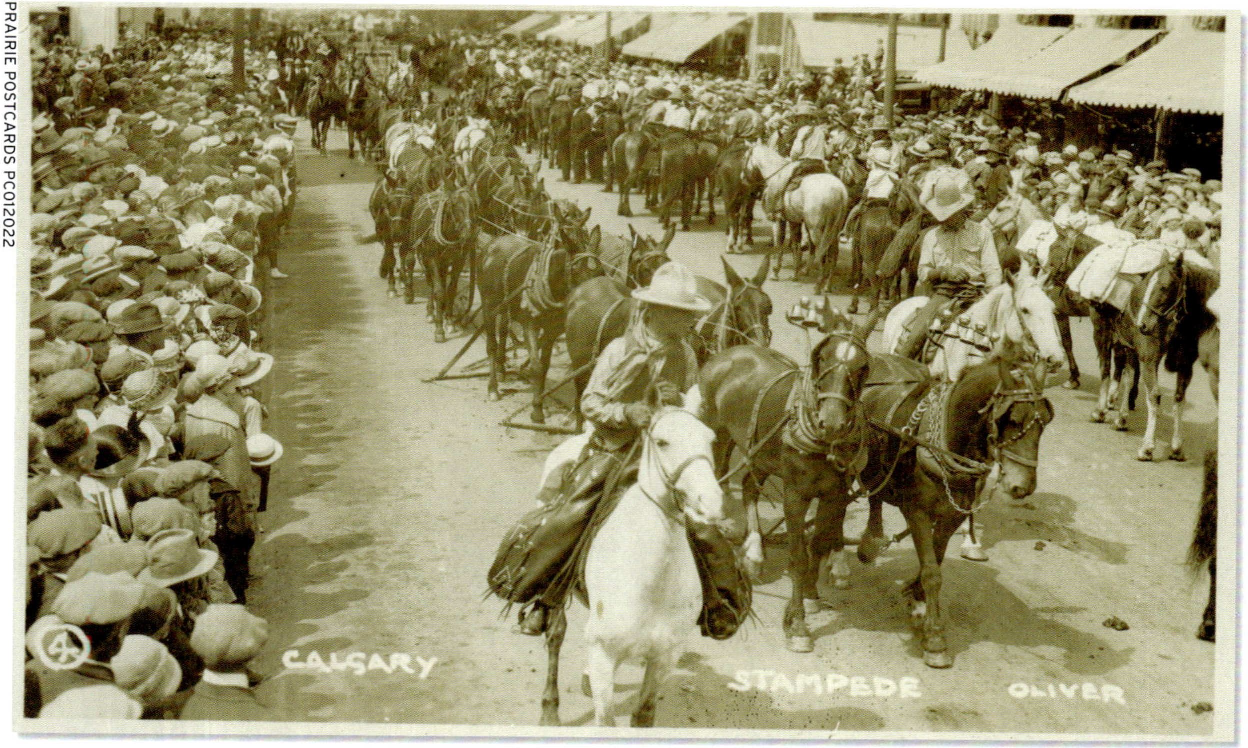

W.J. Oliver caught the famous occasion when Slim Moorehouse drove a new world-record team of 36 horses and mules in the 1925 Calgary Stampede parade.

PC024306

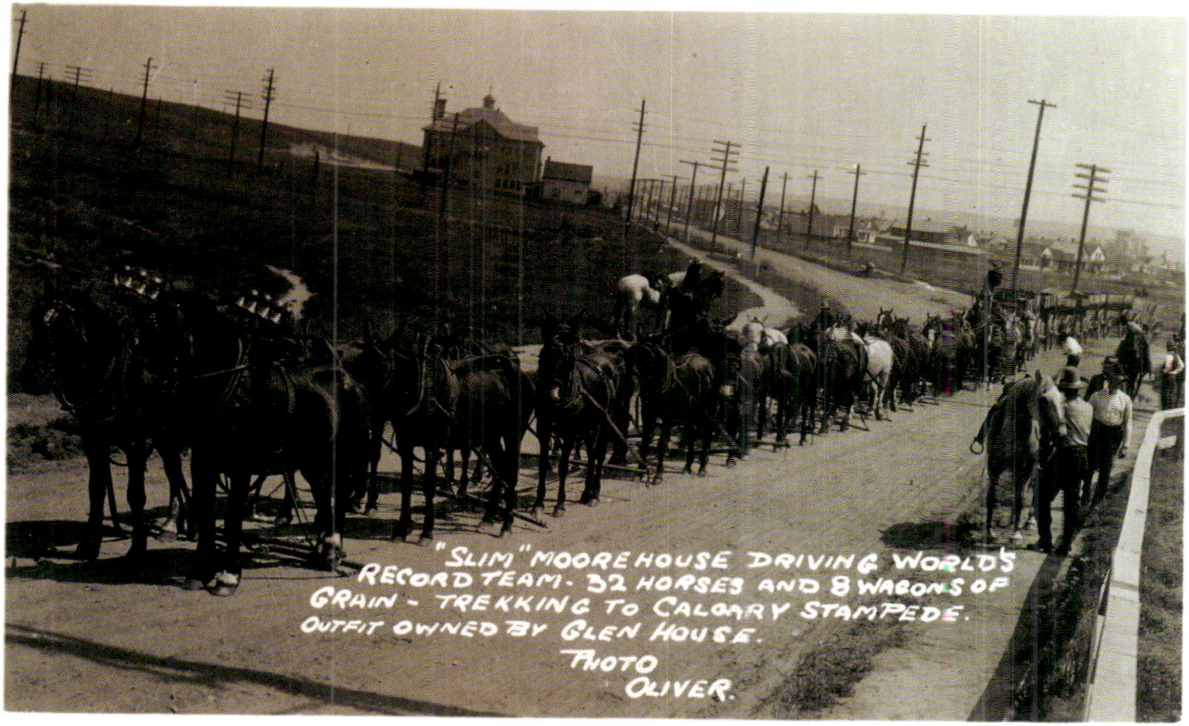

Slim Moorehouse driving world-record mixed team of 32 mules and horses en route to the Stampede.

PRAIRIE POSTCARDS PC006168

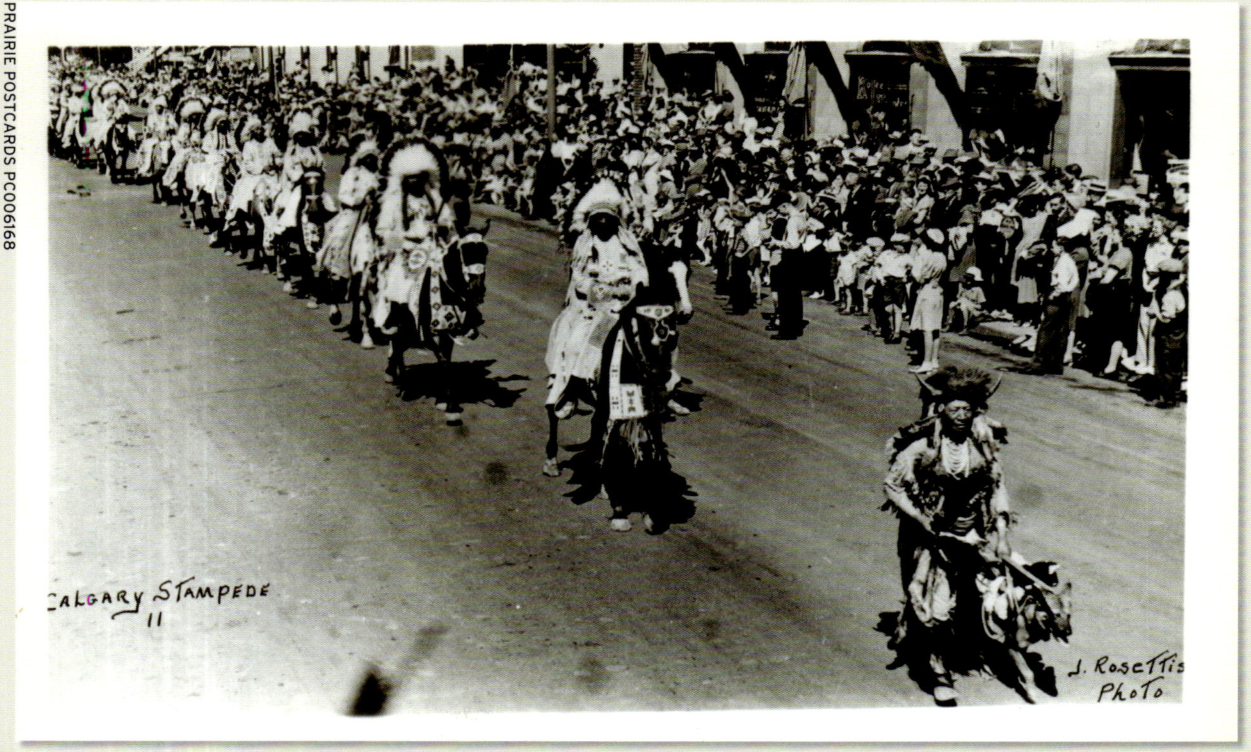

This Rosettis image shows Stoney riders led by Tatanga Mani (Walking Buffalo) at the height of his fame.

PRAIRIE POSTCARDS PC006172

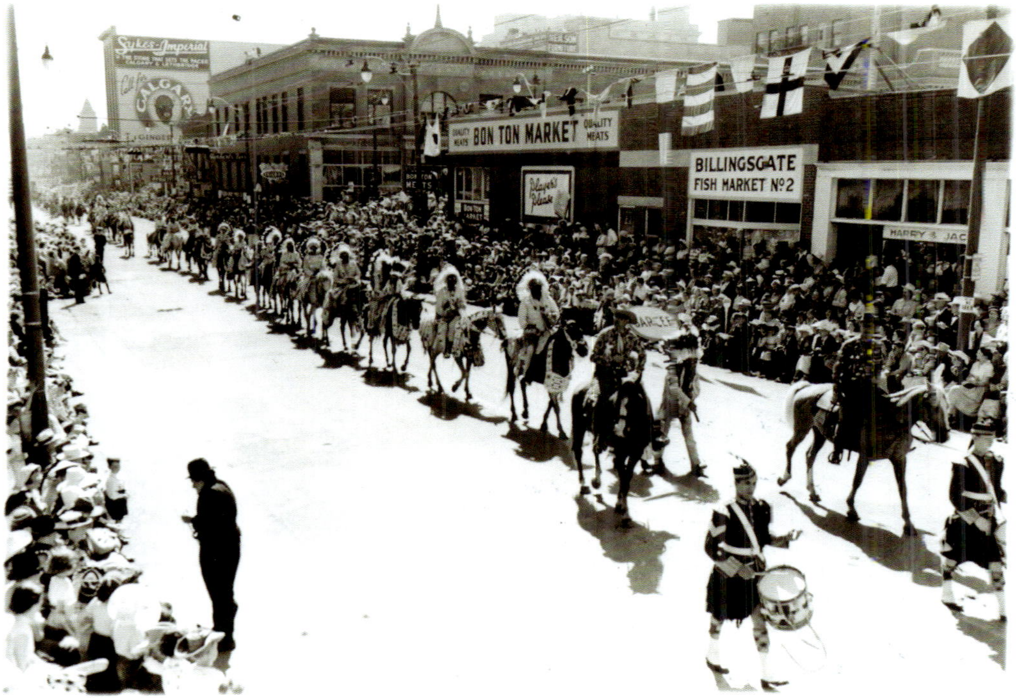

The First Nations formed a vibrant section of the first postwar Calgary Stampede parade in 1919.

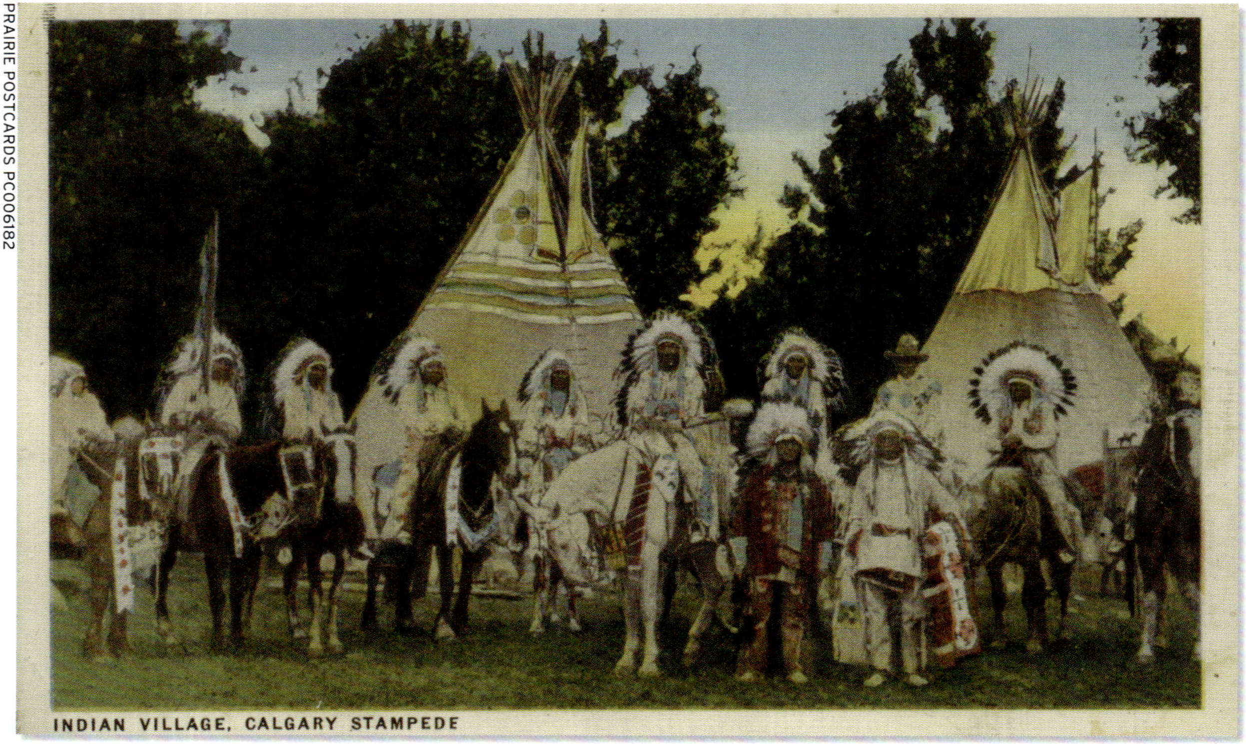

The colourful Indian Village at the Calgary Stampede was portrayed in this view of Blackfoot riders in full regalia. Postmarked 1940, this card is from the Canadian Art Deeptone series for Alberta News Ltd. of Calgary.

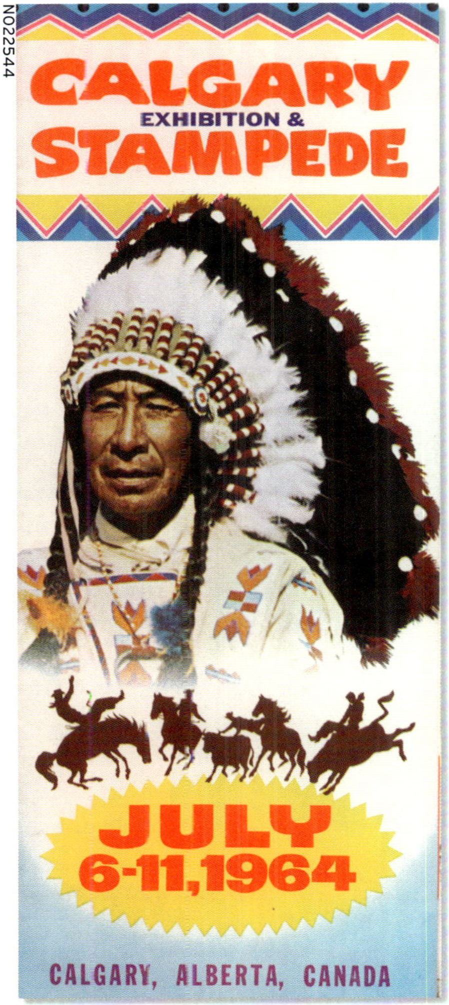

NO22544

Stampede Brochure 1964

PRAIRIE POSTCARDS PC006174

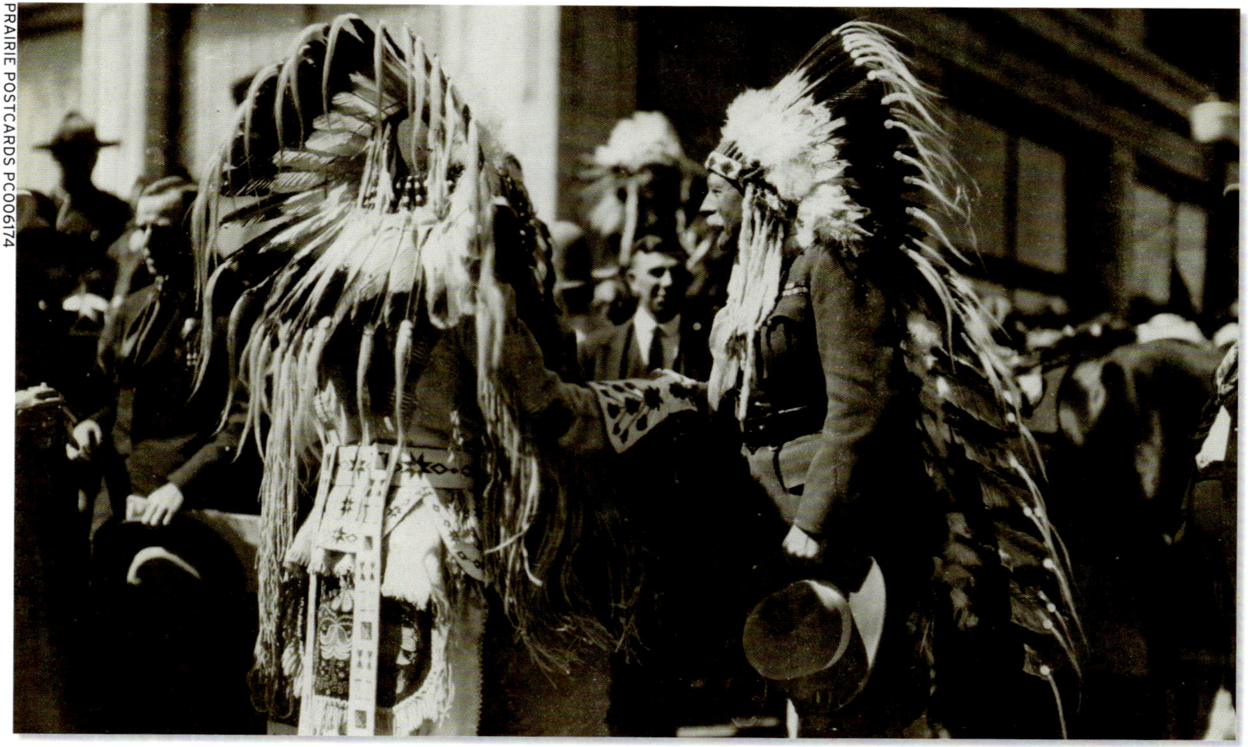

Field Marshal Earl Haig was named an honorary chief of the Sarcee nation during his visit to the Calgary Stampede in 1925.

PC024383A

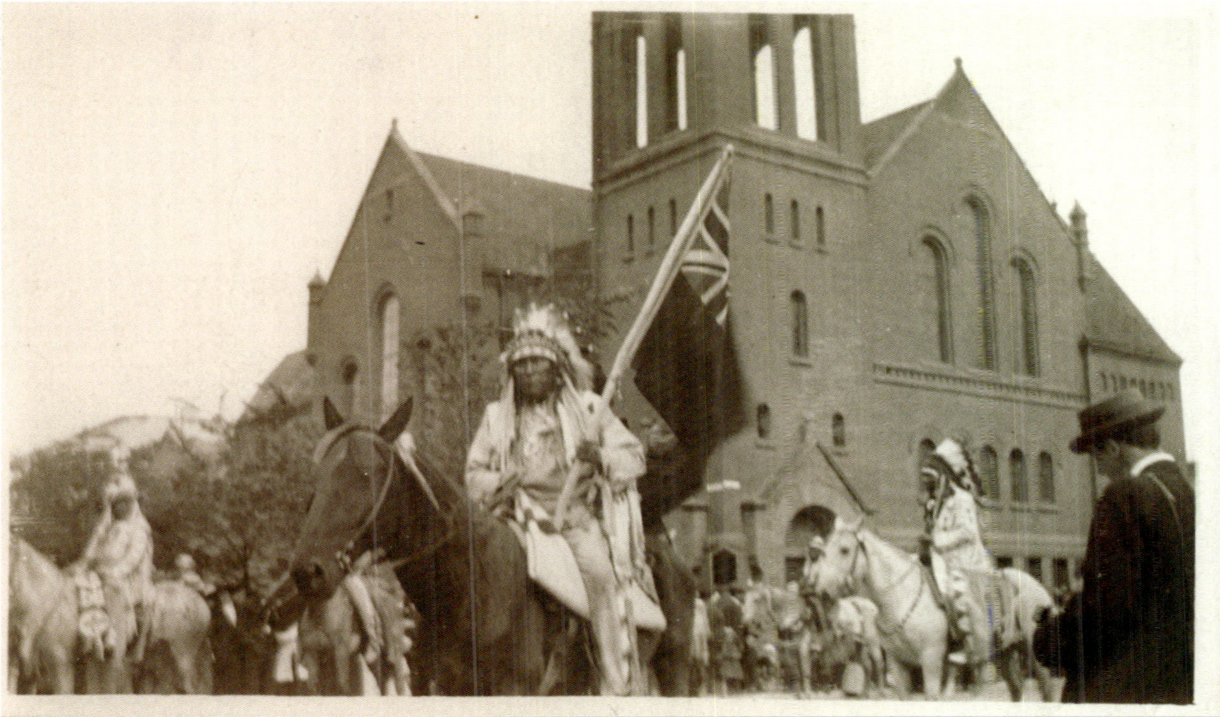

Aboriginal riders and church

VPC024383C

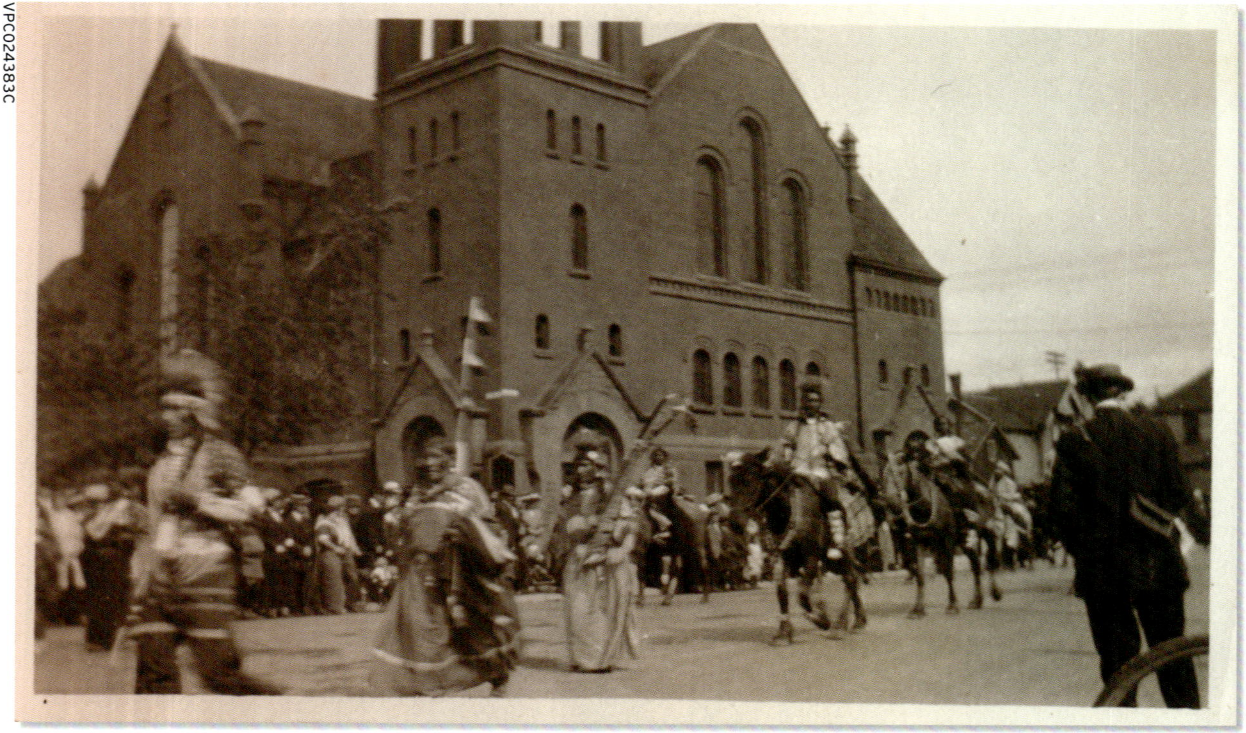

Aboriginal riders and church

PC024383B

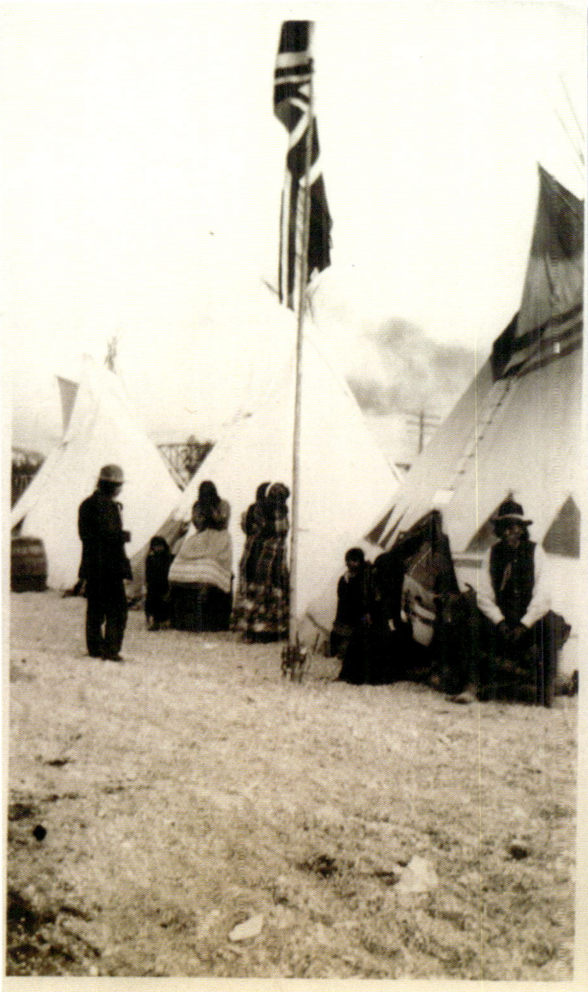

Aboriginal camp

PRAIRIE POSTCARDS PC006175

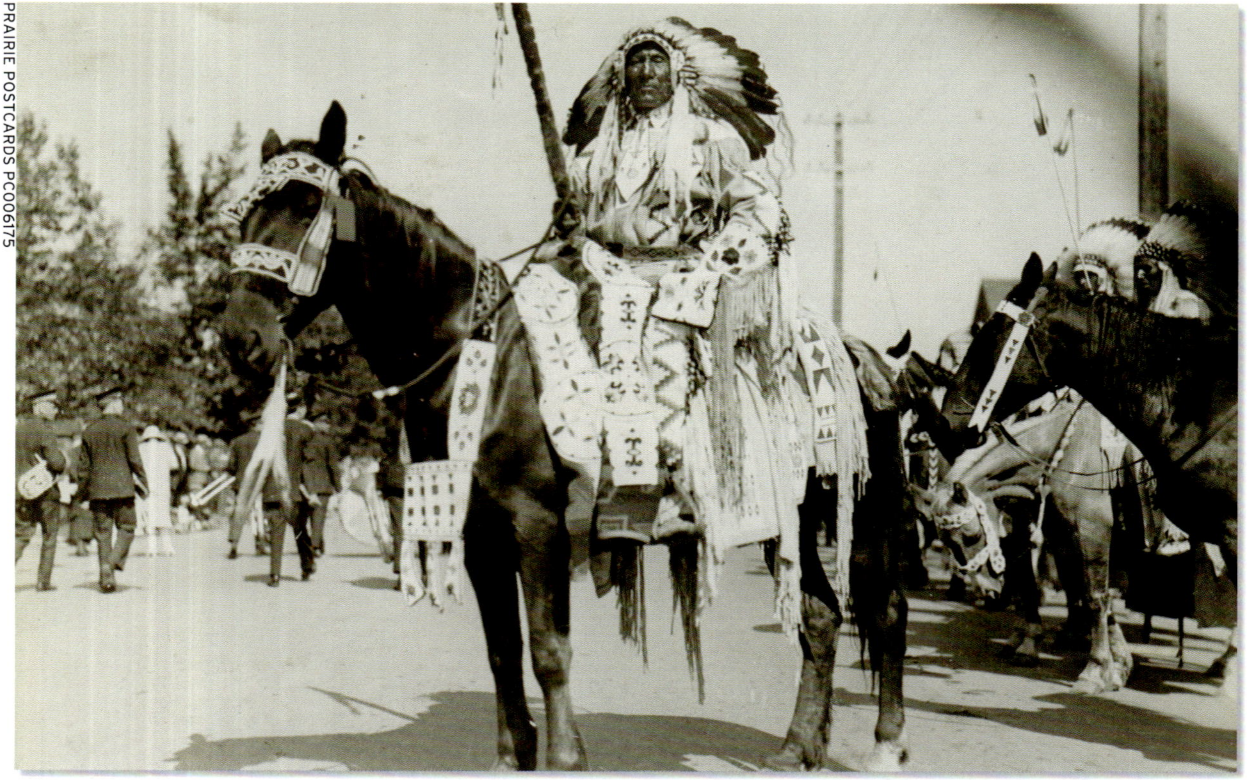

Aboriginal riders were an important part of the Calgary Stampede throughout the 1930s.

PRAIRIE POSTCARDS PC006171

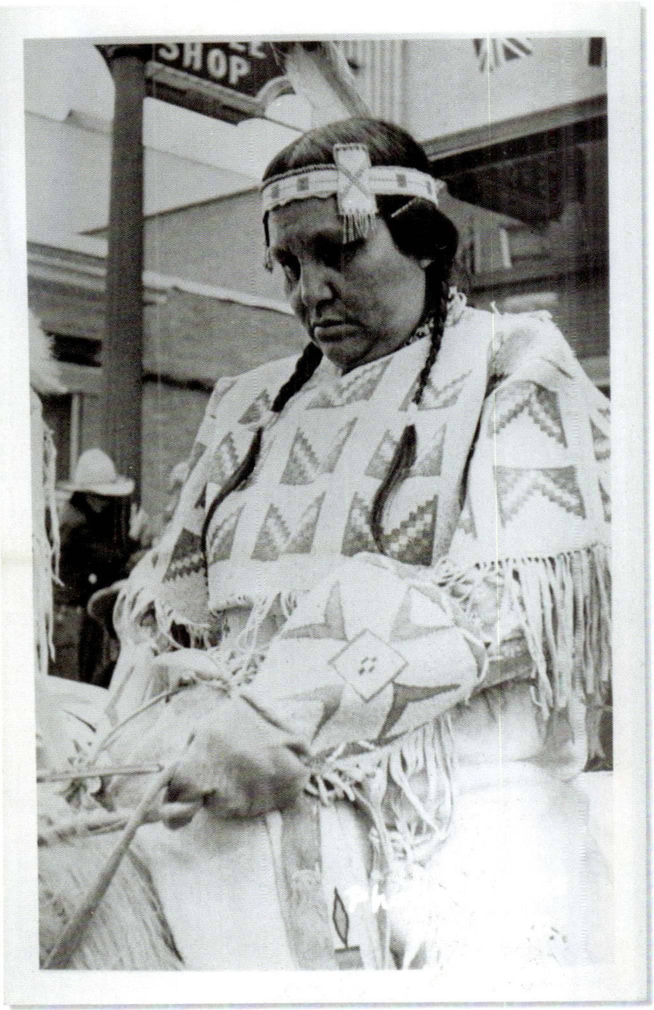

An aboriginal rider in a Calgary Stampede parade.

PRAIRIE POSTCARDS PC006165

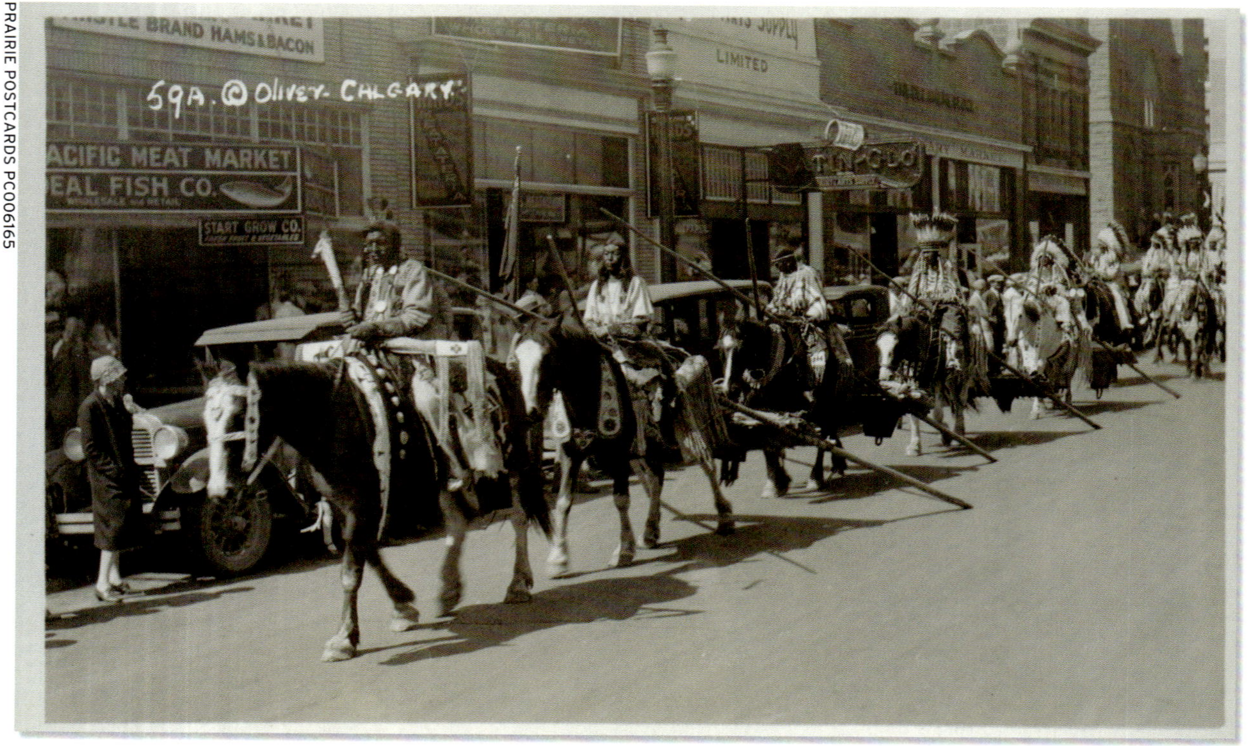

Aboriginal riders pull several travois along a Calgary street in a Stampede parade during the 1920s. Part of the W.J. Oliver postcard series.

PRAIRIE POSTCARDS PC006180

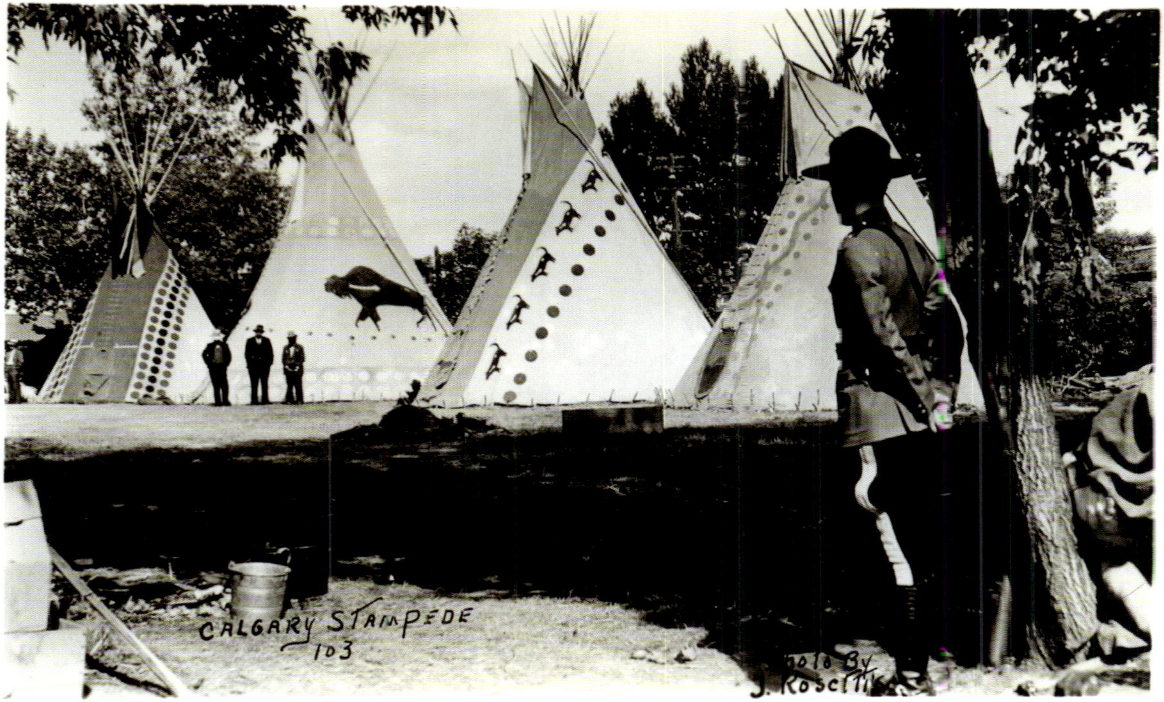

Rosettis Studio produced this iconic image of the Indian Village, with an RCMP constable overlooking the scene in full dress uniform.

PRAIRIE POSTCARDS PC018805

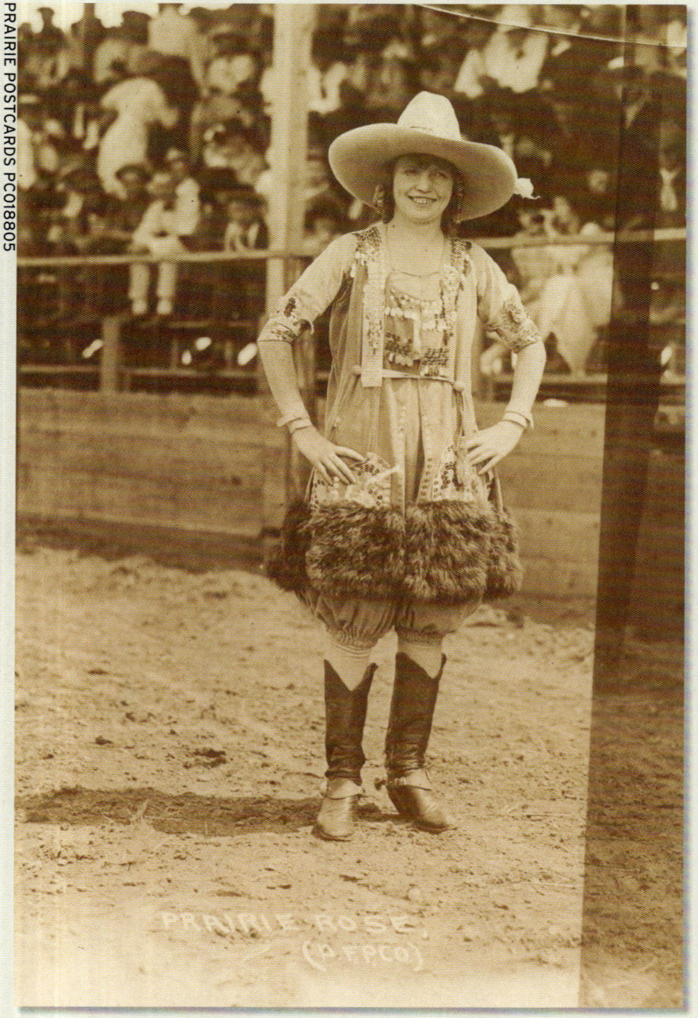

Prairie Rose

PC024391

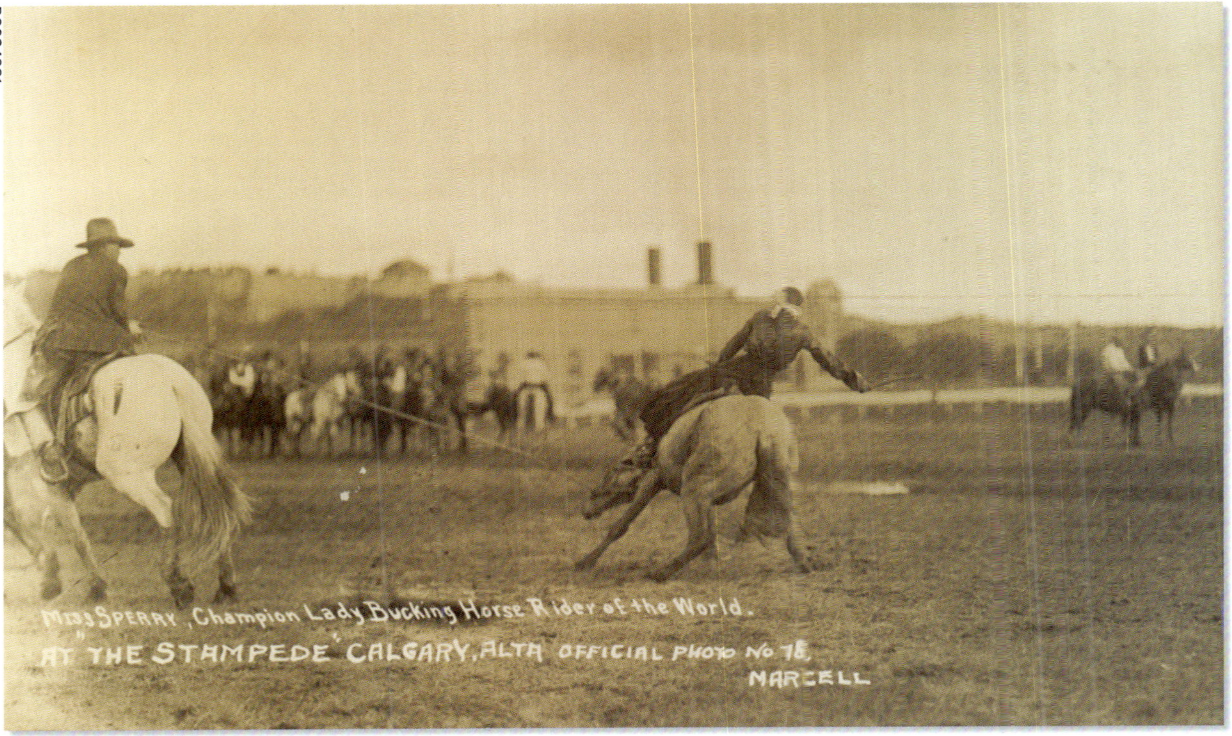

Miss Sperry, champion lady bucking horse rider, Calgary Stampede

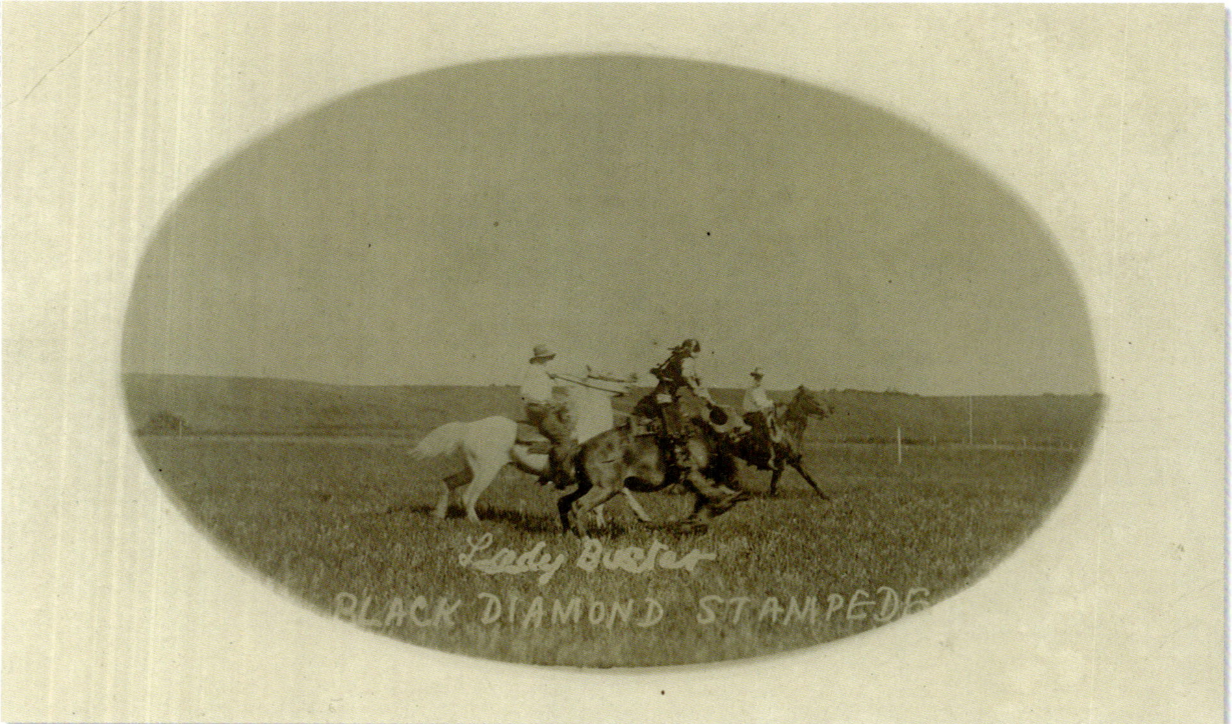

A "lady buster" at the Black Diamond Stampede, published in Calgary by the Chazin Studio during the 1920s.

PC024543

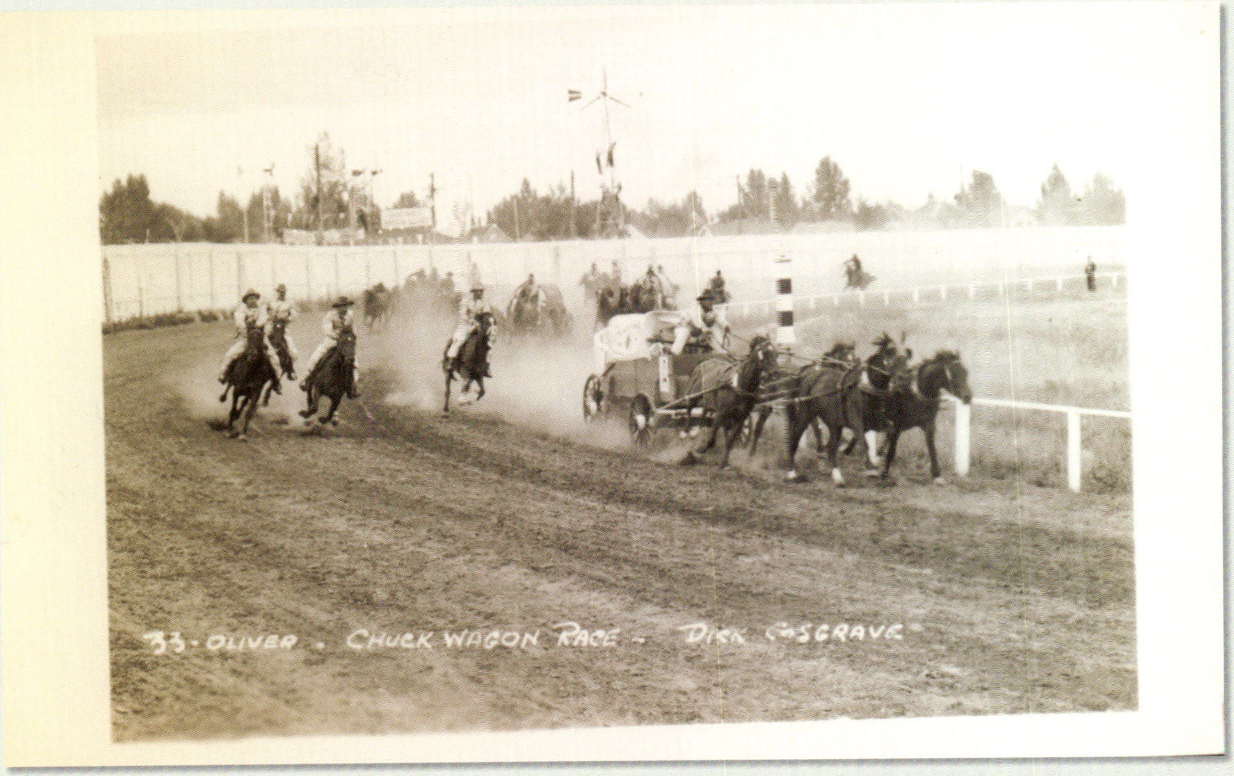

Dick Cosgrave wagon

PRAIRIE POSTCARDS PC006323

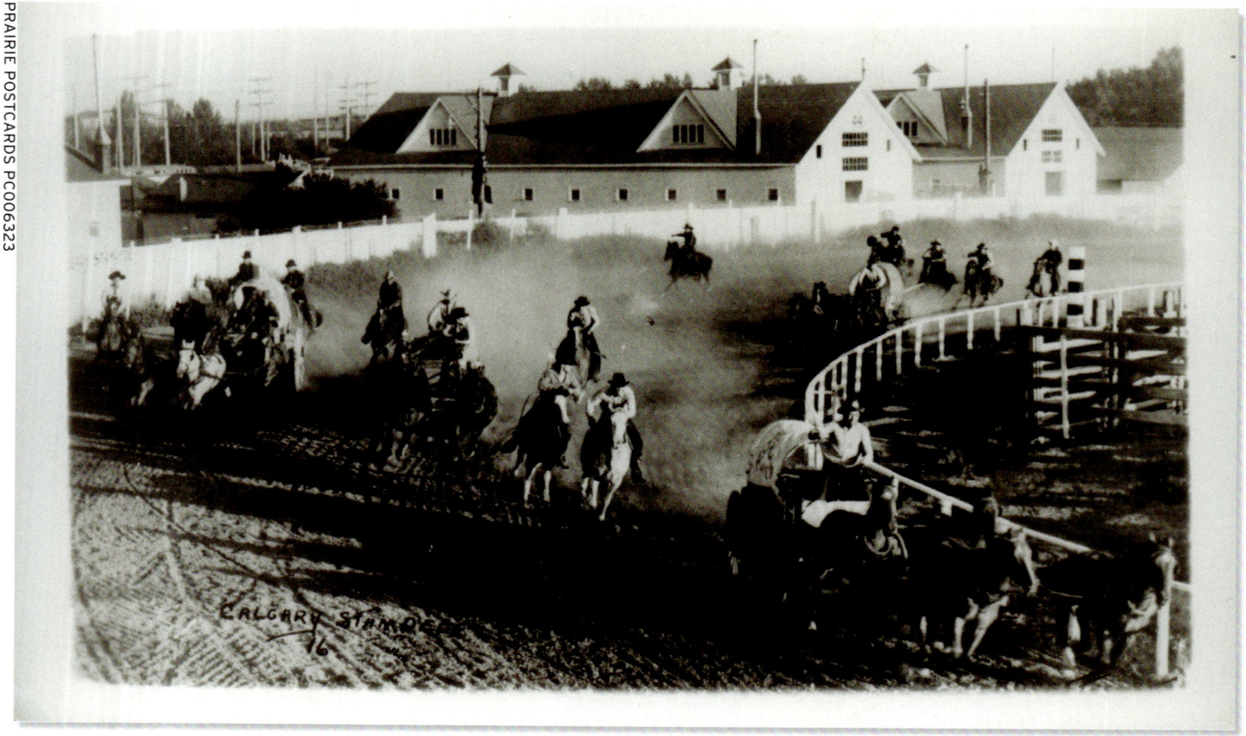

The chuckwagon races are probably the trademark event of the Stampede. Many feel that the speed, dust, noise and sometimes chaos are hard to beat as a spectator sport.

PC018806

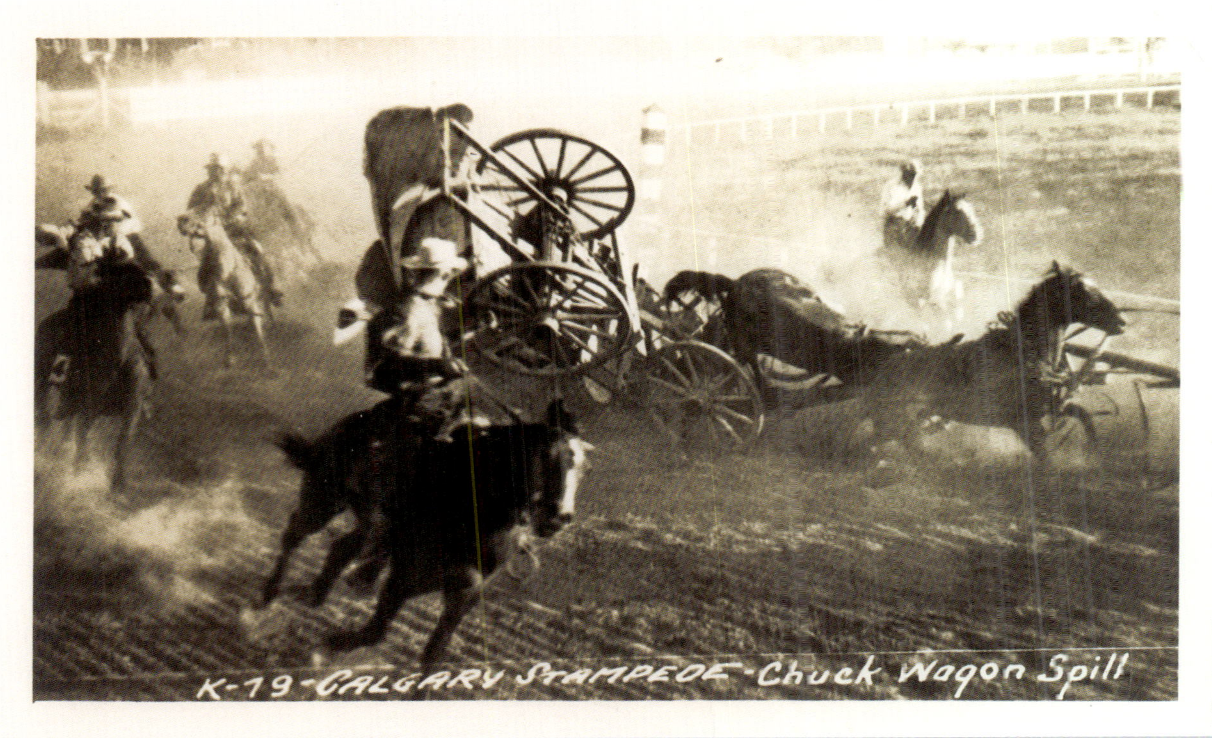

Calgary Stampede chuckwagon spill

PC023625

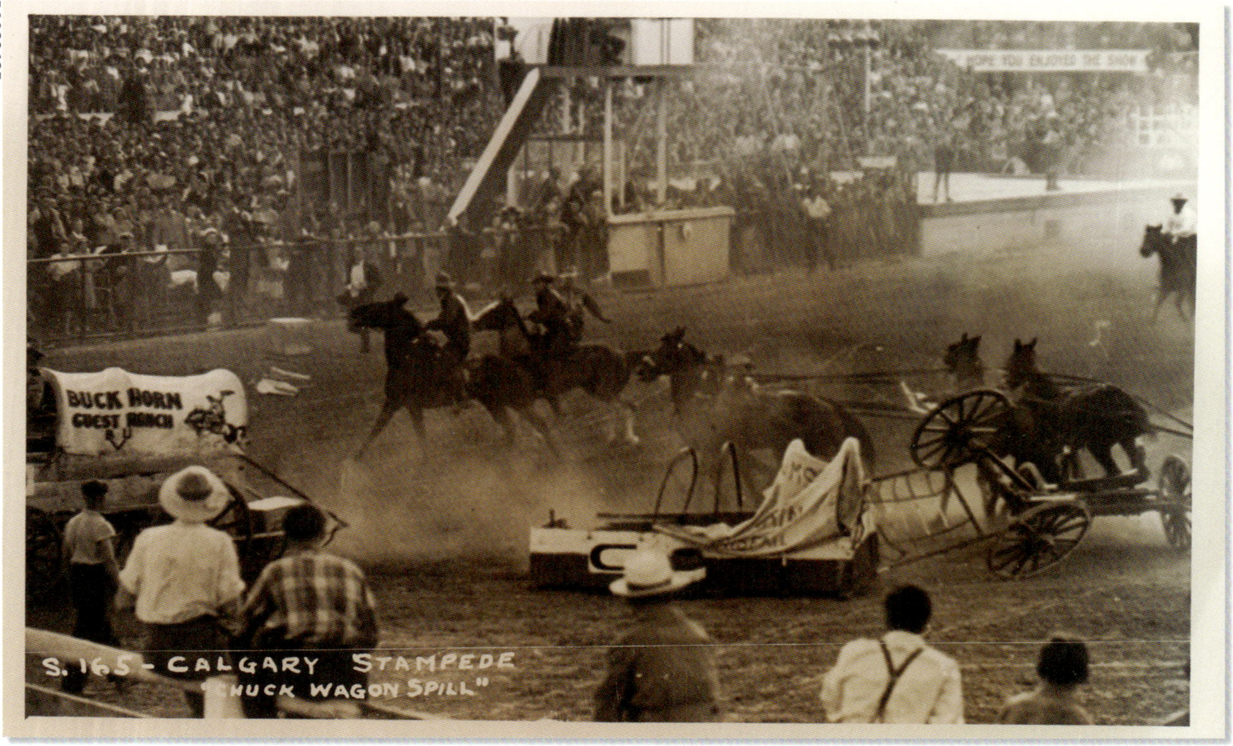

Calgary Stampede chuckwagon spill

PC023624

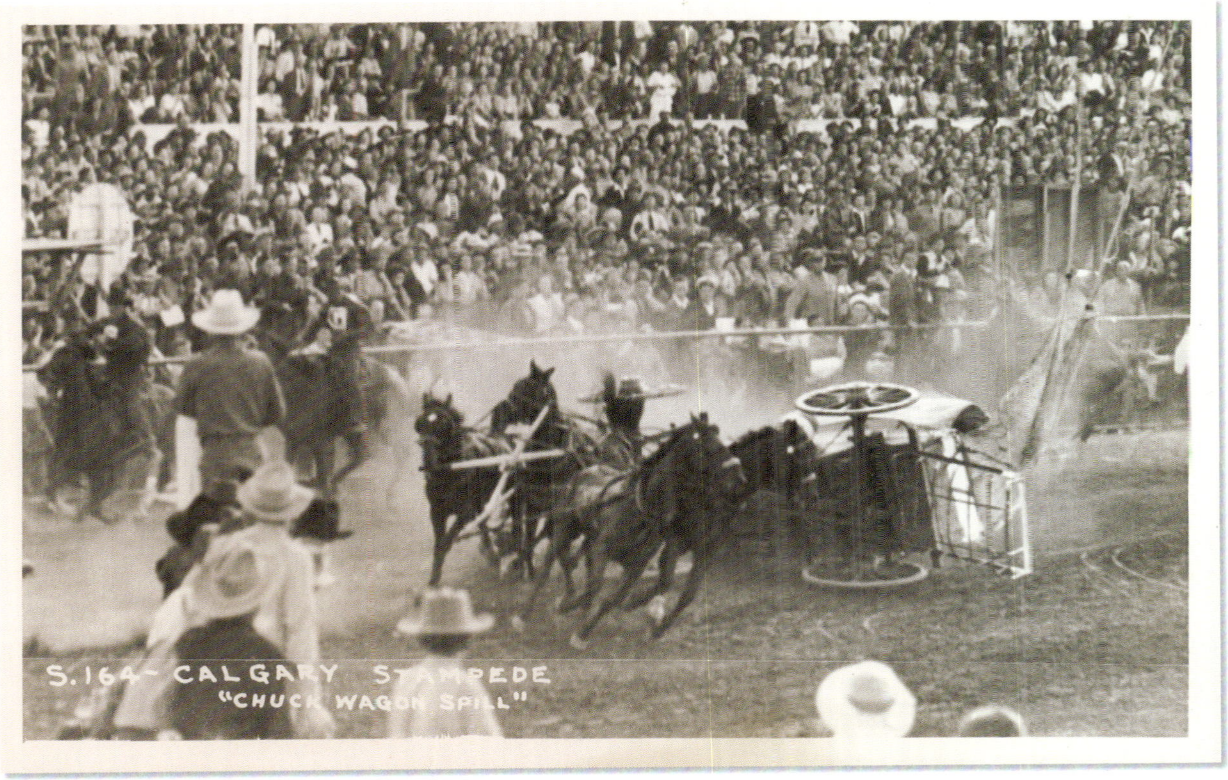

Calgary Stampede chuckwagon spill

PRAIRIE POSTCARDS PC006195

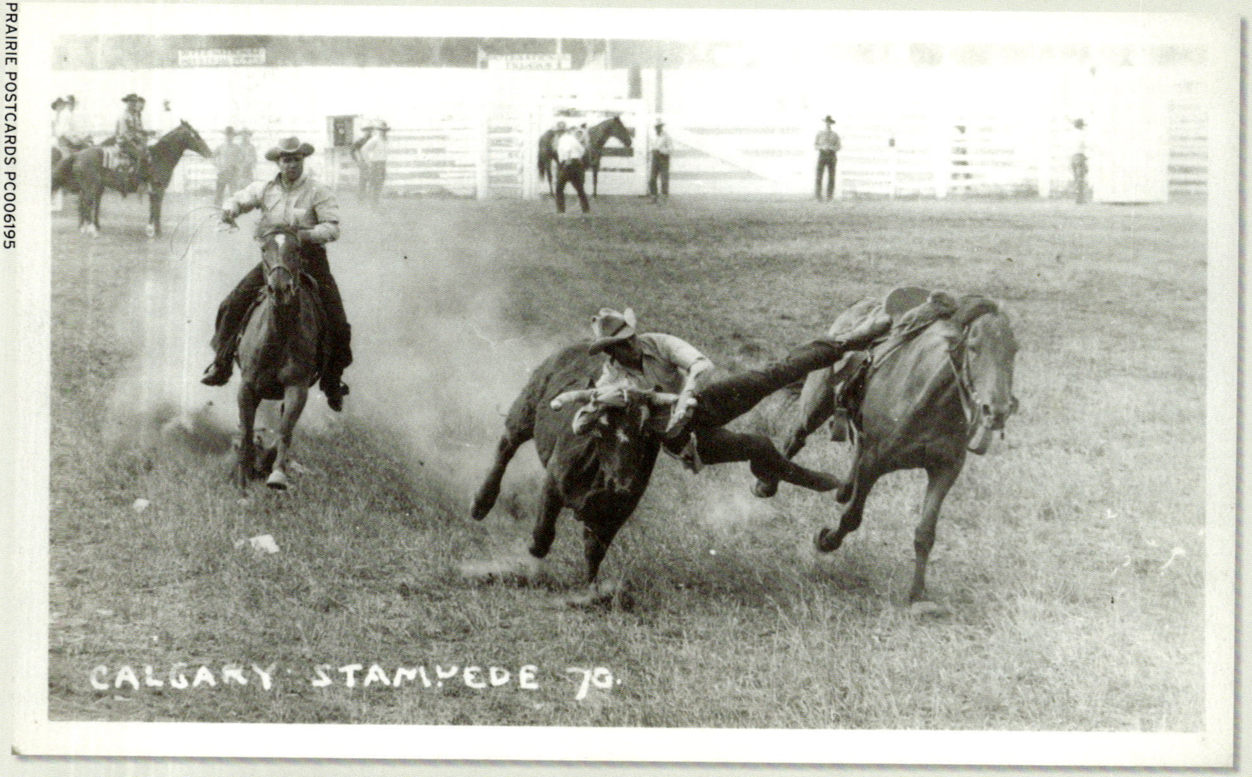

Bulldogging was an ever-popular event, despite the early uproar about the blood-spattered longhorn events in the first Stampedes.

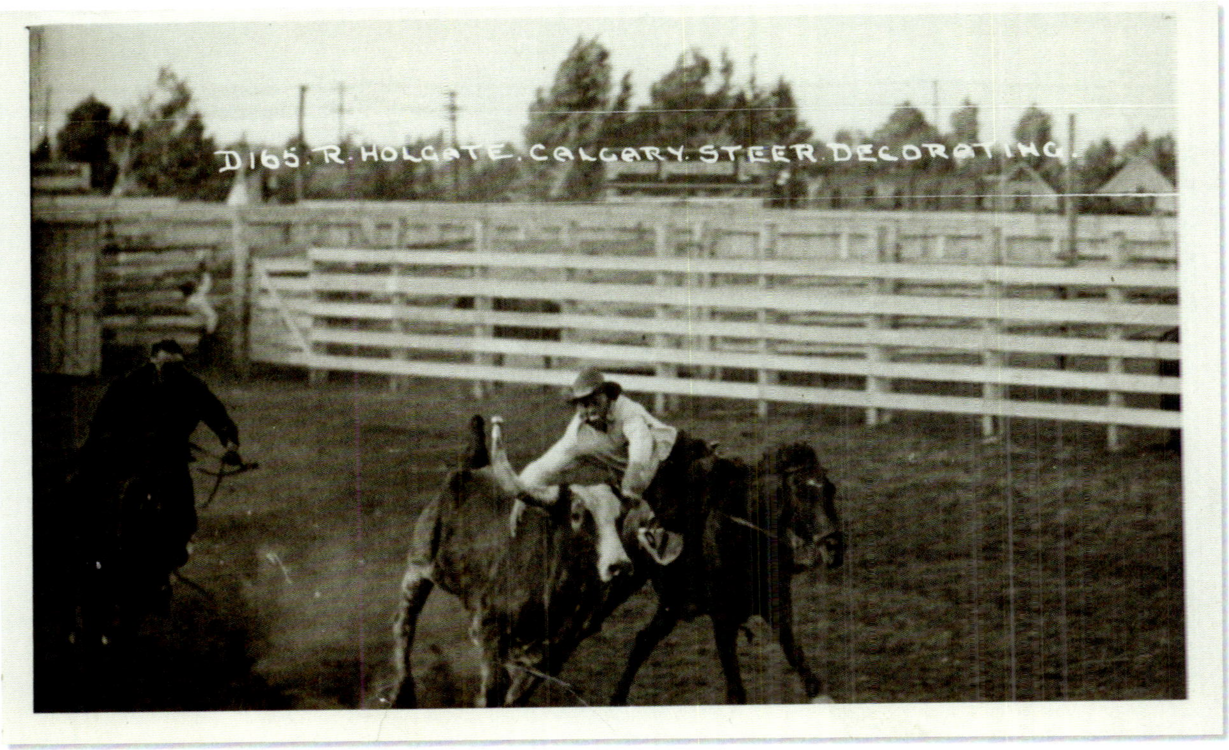

PRAIRIE POSTCARDS PC012025

R. Holgate demonstrates the fine art of steer decorating at the 1932 Stampede. Notice the balls on the long-horn tips to prevent too much injury to the decorator as he flies through the air toward his galloping target.

PC015629

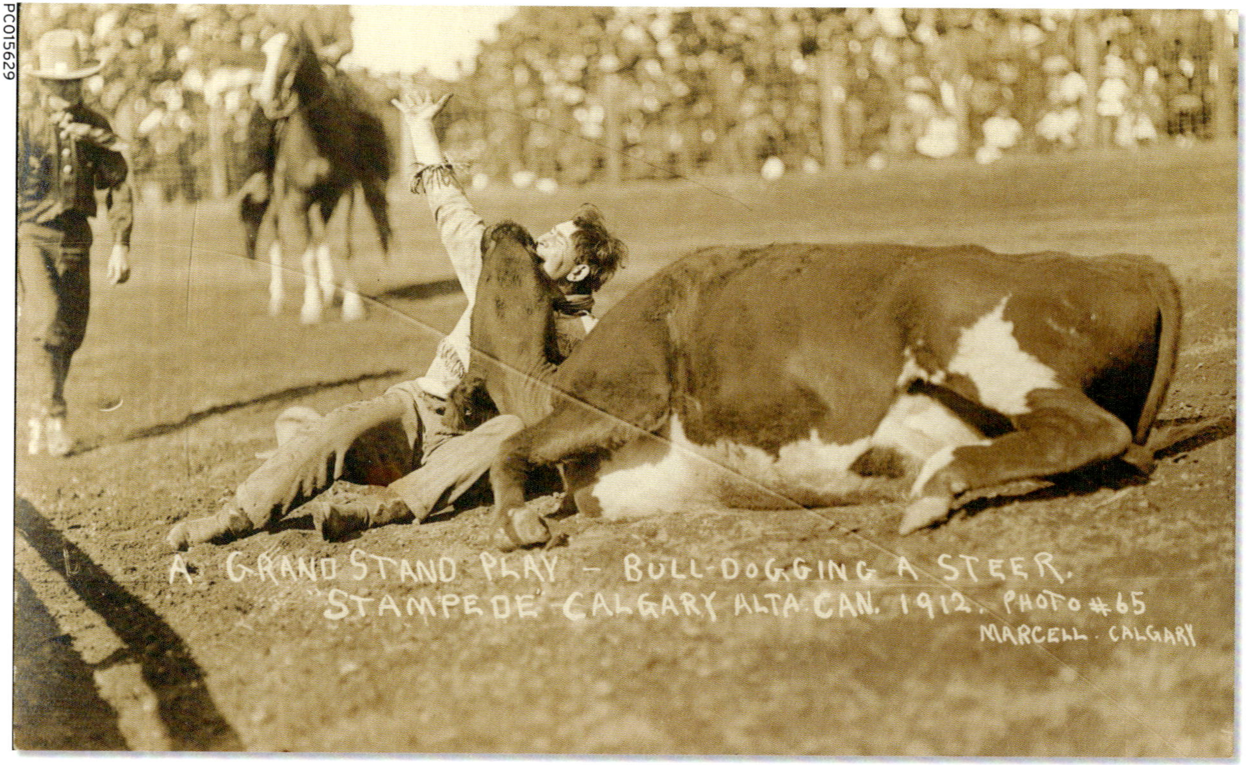

A grandstand play, bulldogging a steer at the Calgary Stampede

PC024594

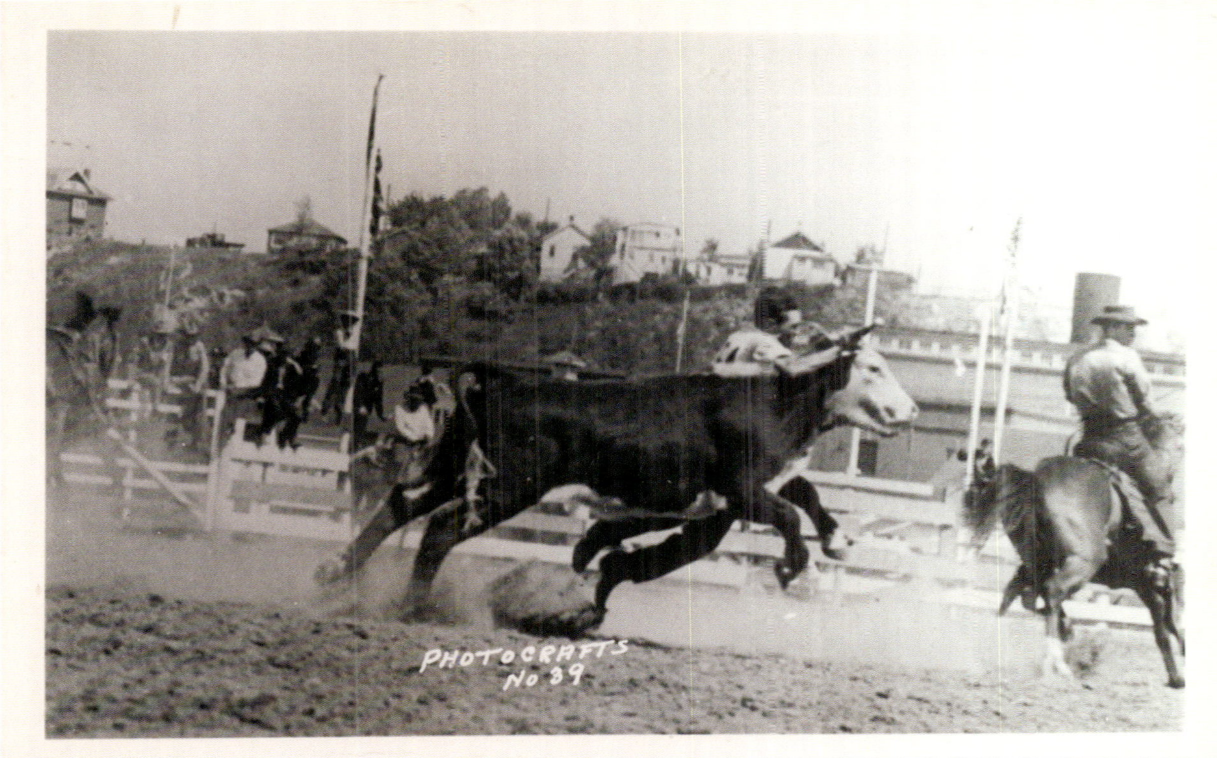

Bulldogging a steer

PC023627

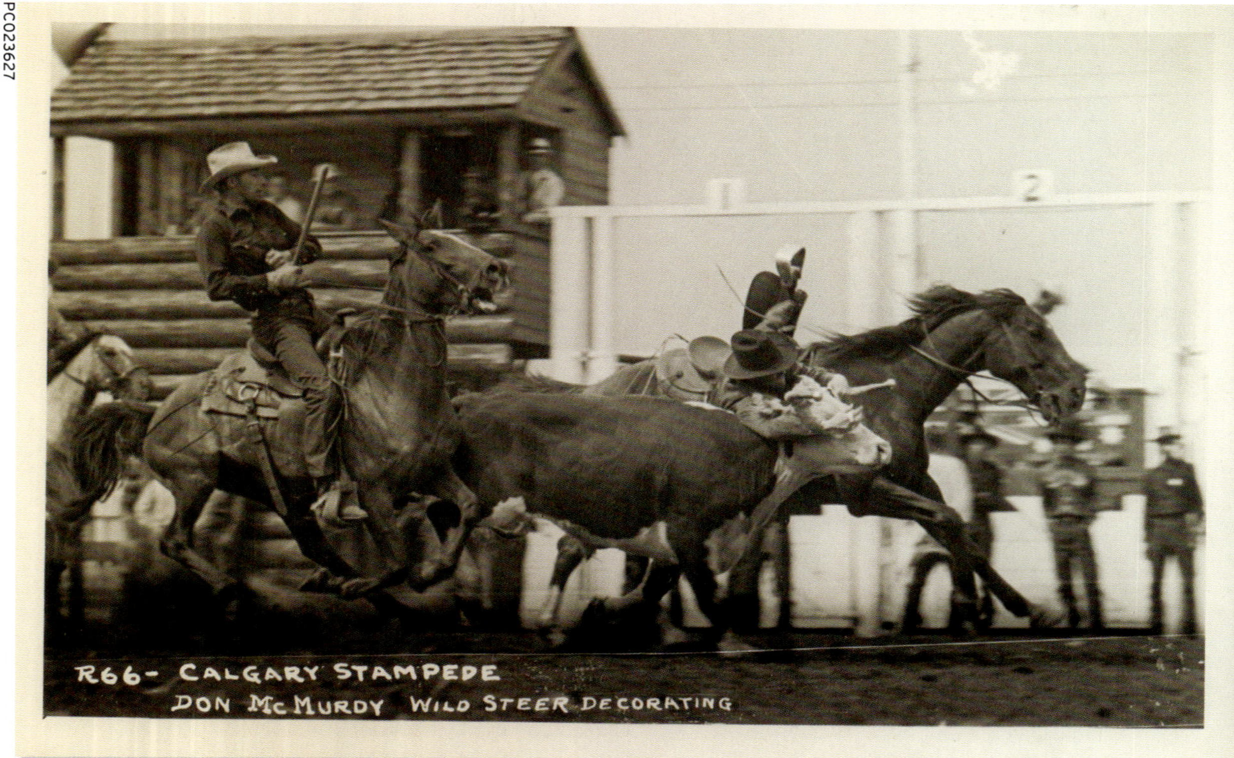

Don McMurdy decorating a wild steer at the Calgary Stampede

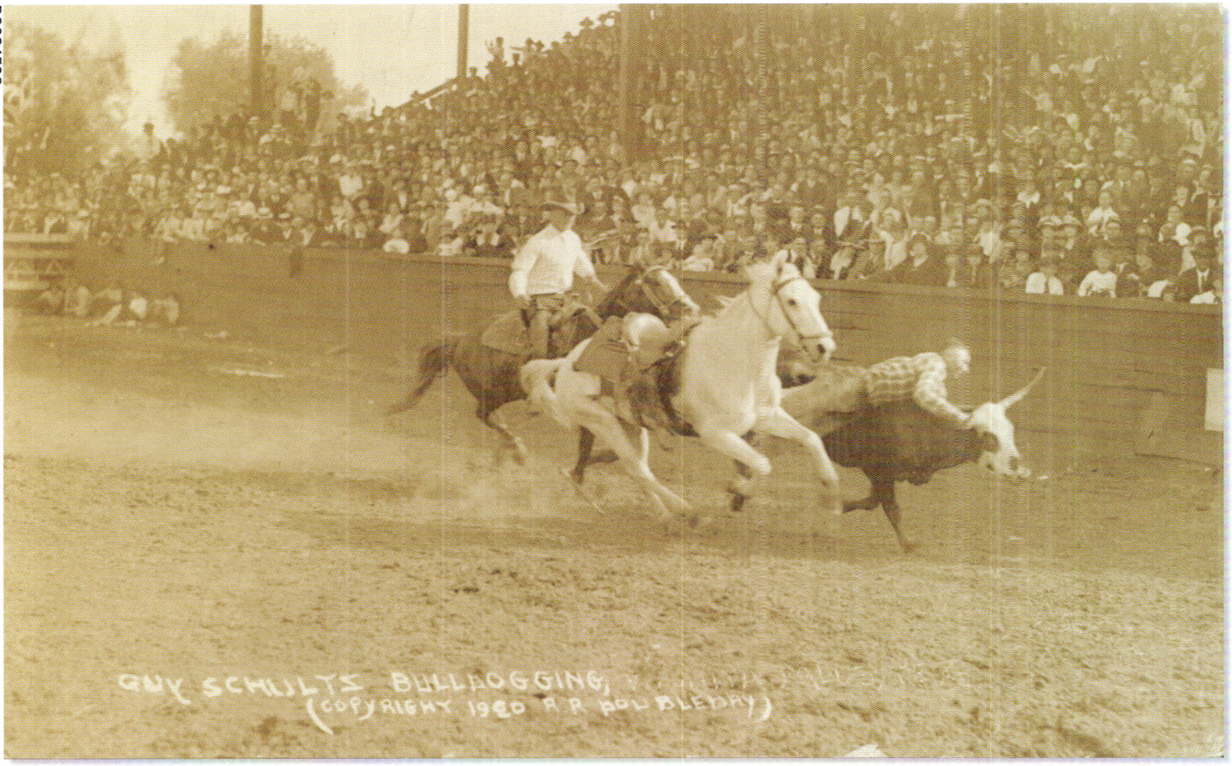

Guy Schultz bulldogging, 1920

PC024566

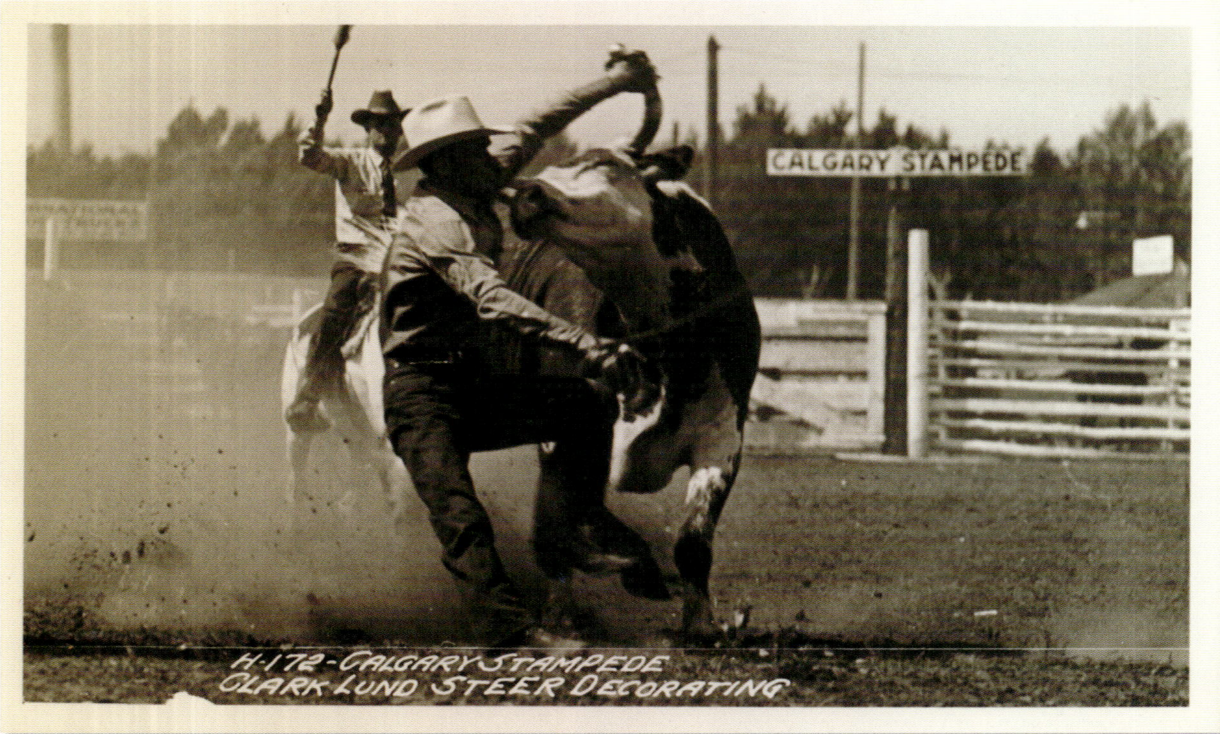

Clark Lund steer decorating, Calgary Stampede

PRAIRIE POSTCARDS PC006200

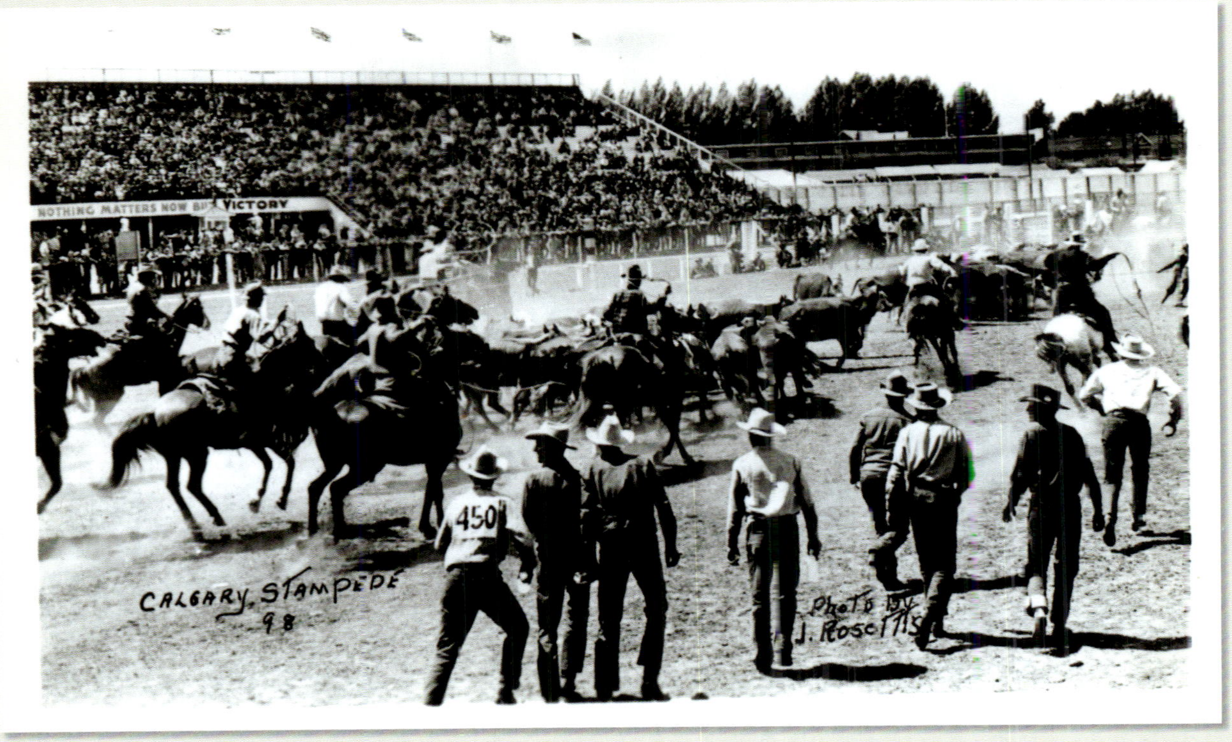

Joe Rosettis captured this great scene of a Calgary Stampede show during the Second World War.

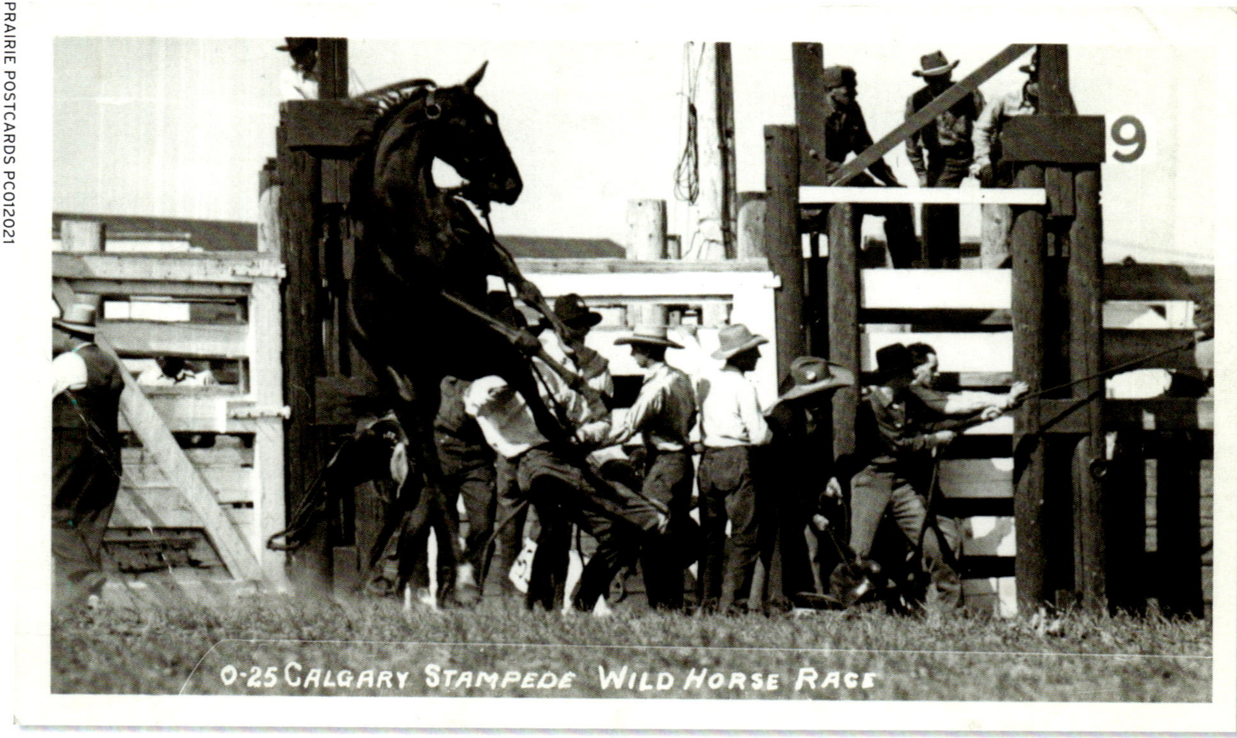

This hectic image of roping mounts for the wild-horse race was published by the Calgary Photo Supply Co. in about 1932.

PRAIRIE POSTCARDS PC006295

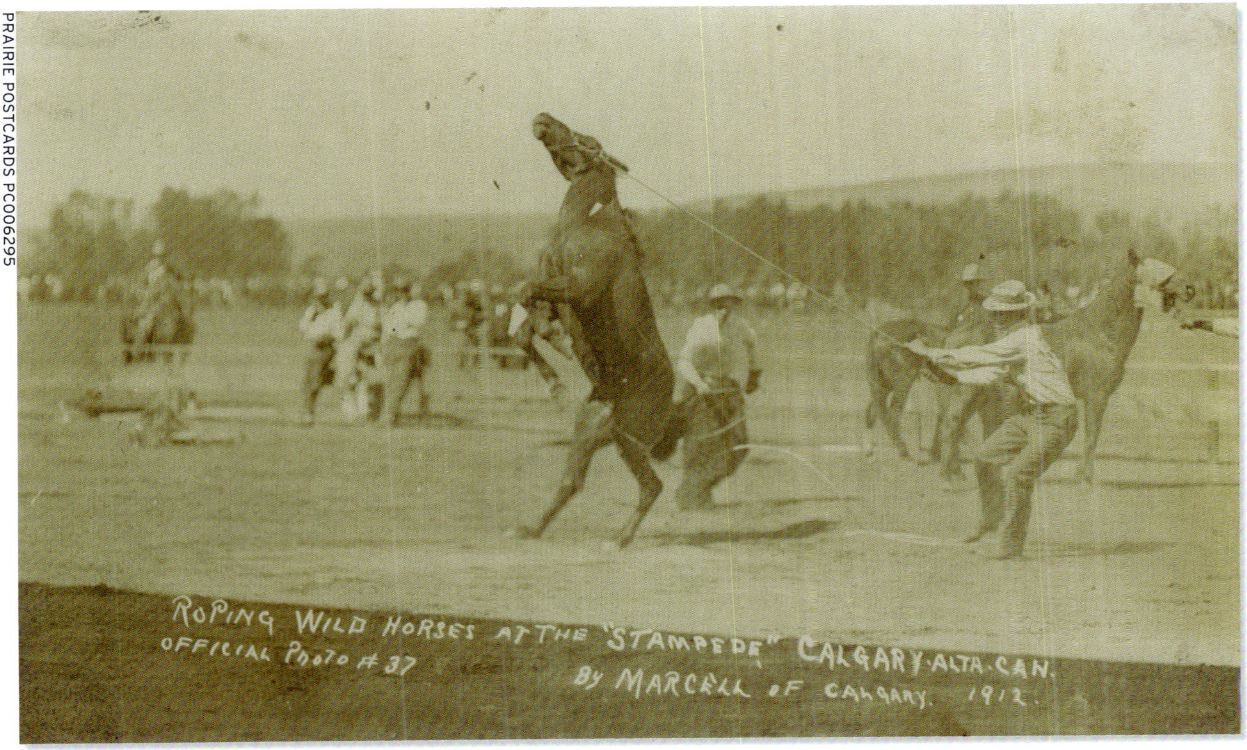

Another classic view of the inaugural Calgary Stampede action in 1912. Marcell of Calgary shows the scramble to rope steeds for the wild-horse race.

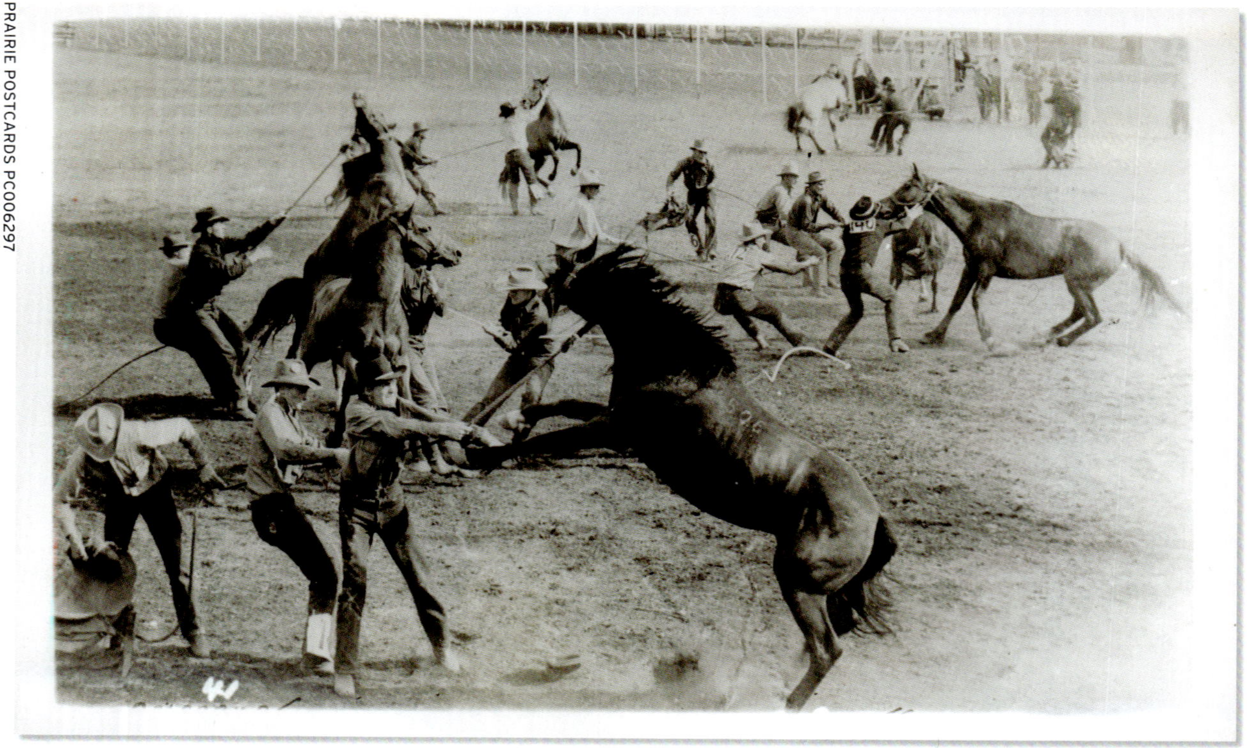

PRAIRIE POSTCARDS PC006297

The wild-horse races have been an integral part of the Stampede from its first days. Despite changes to the rules, it has remained wild and woolly.

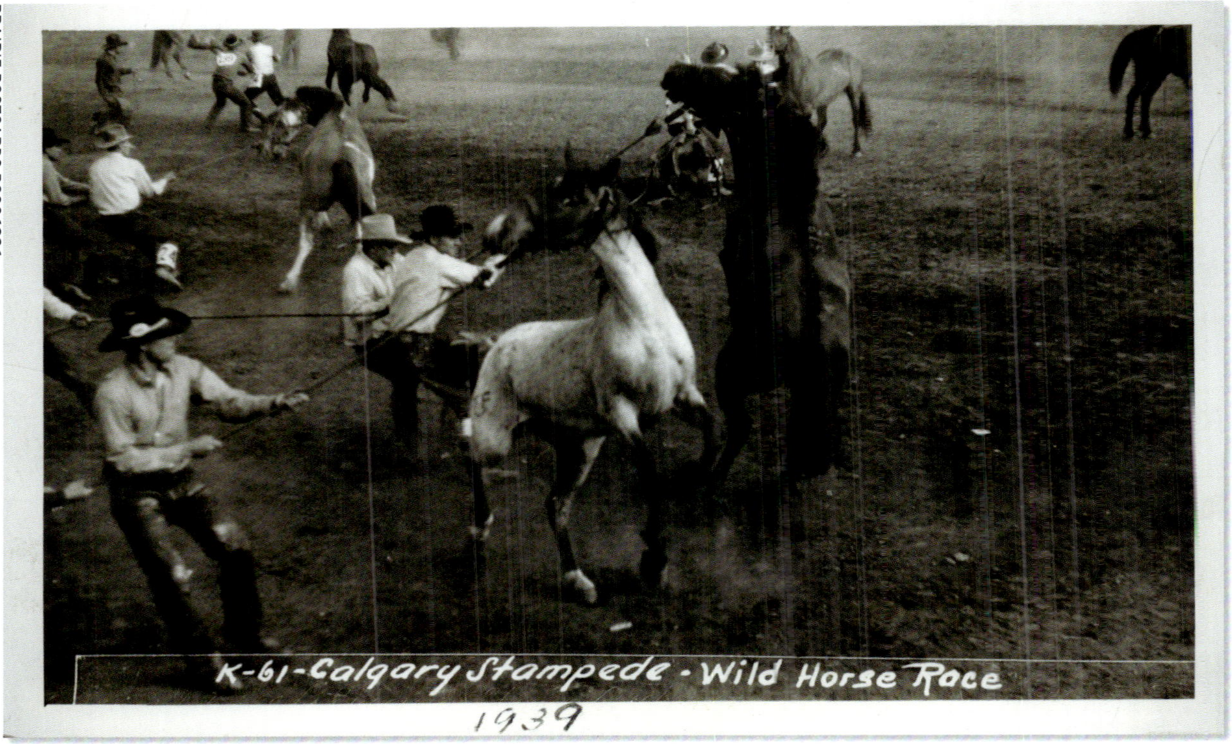

PRAIRIE POSTCARDS PC006296

Another in the Calgary Photo Supply Co. series captures the wild and dusty melee as horses are roped for the wild-horse race in 1939.

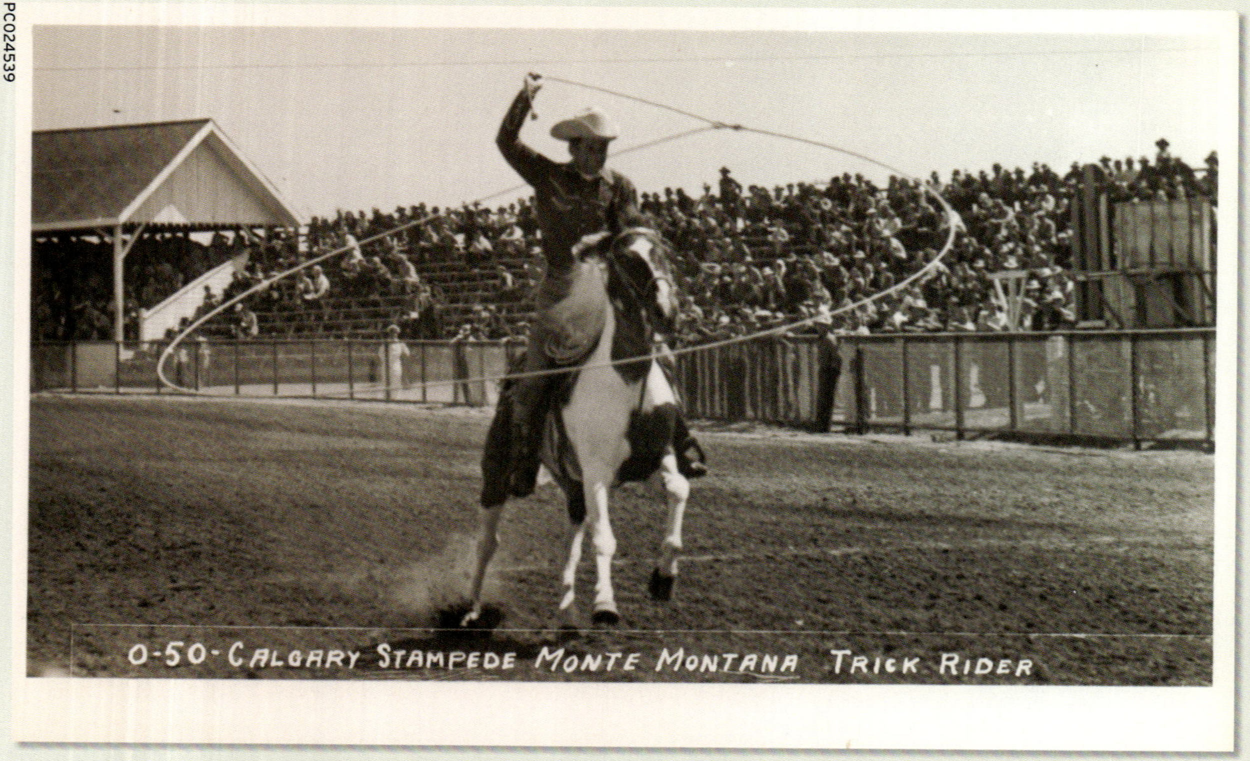

Monte Montana, a trick rider at the Calgary Stampede

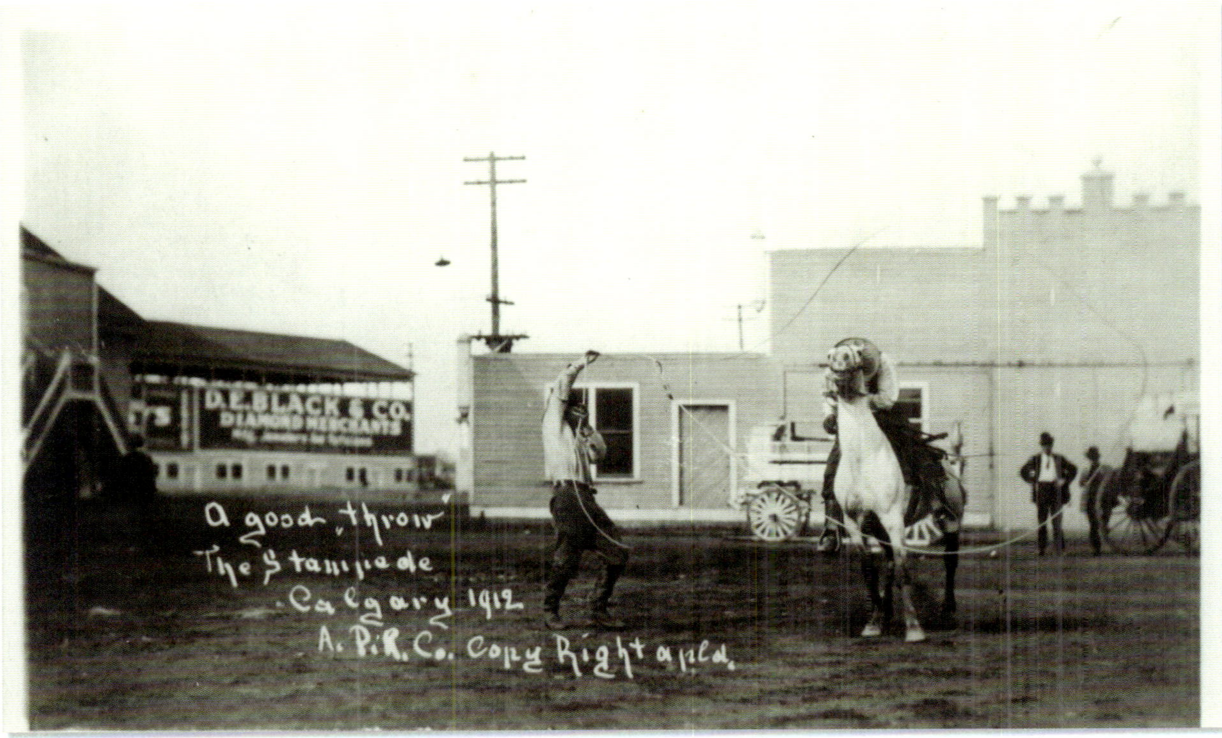

"A good throw" by a trick roper performing for his pals at the 1912 Calgary Stampede. The A.P.K. Co. produced this postcard.

PRAIRIE POSTCARDS PC006301

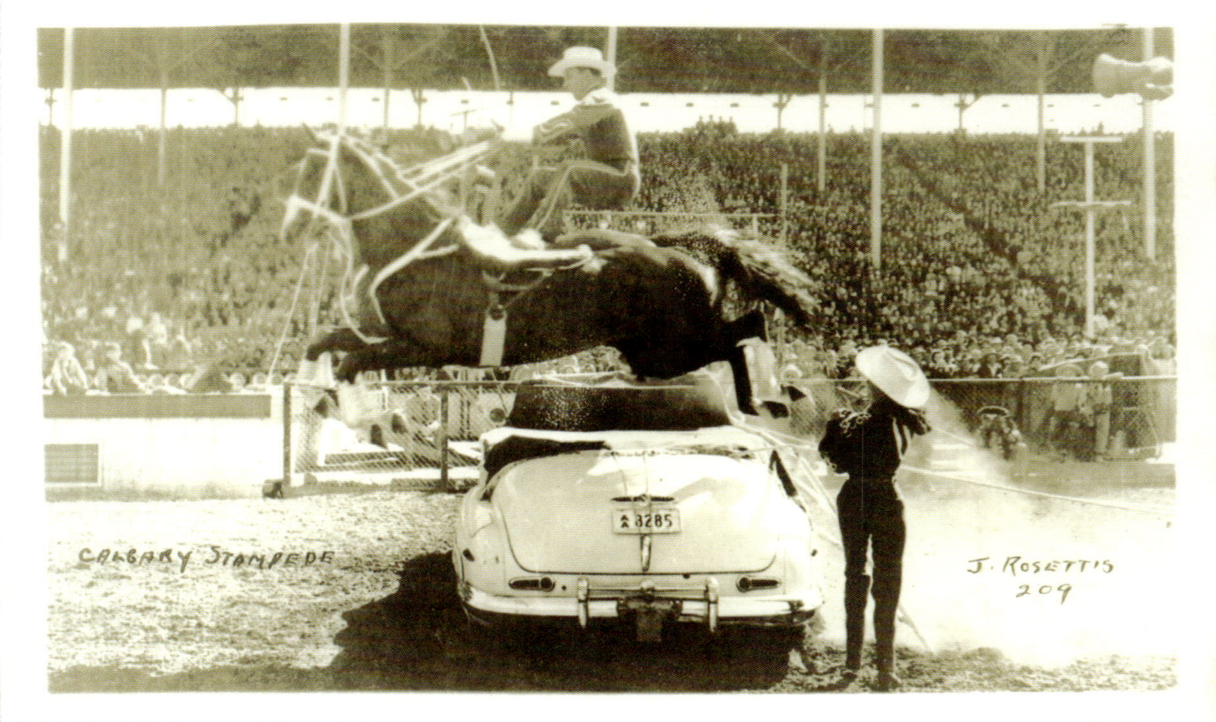

Trick riding at the Stampede, circa 1948. Another of the excellent Joe Rosettis images capturing the excitement of the Stampede shows.

PC024541

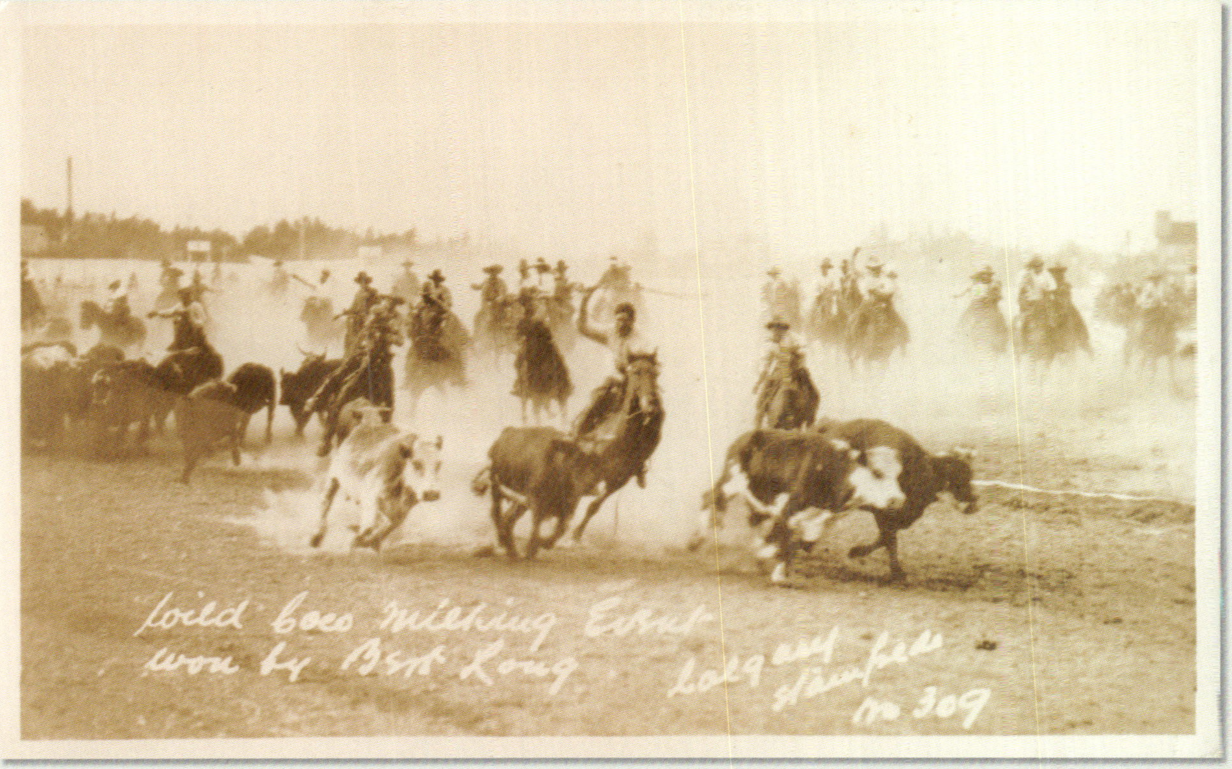

Wild-cow milking at the Calgary Stampede, won that year by Bert Long

PC024545

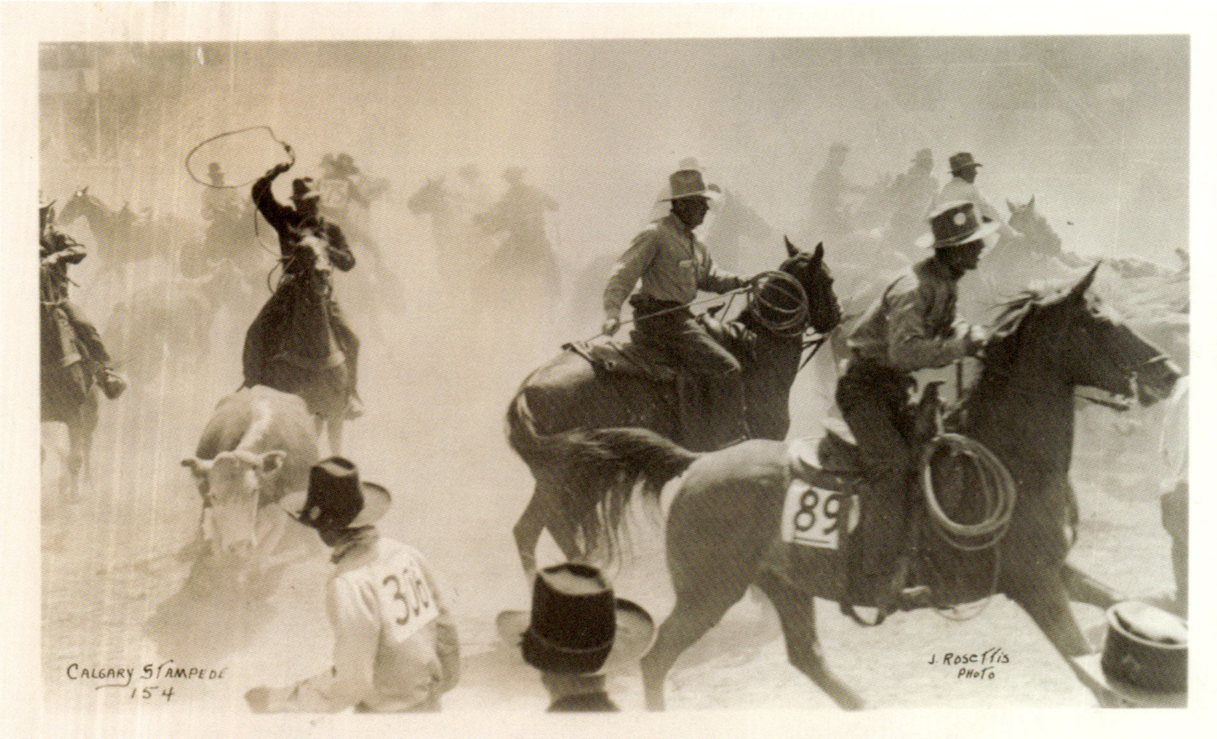

Roping cattle, Calgary Stampede

PC024589

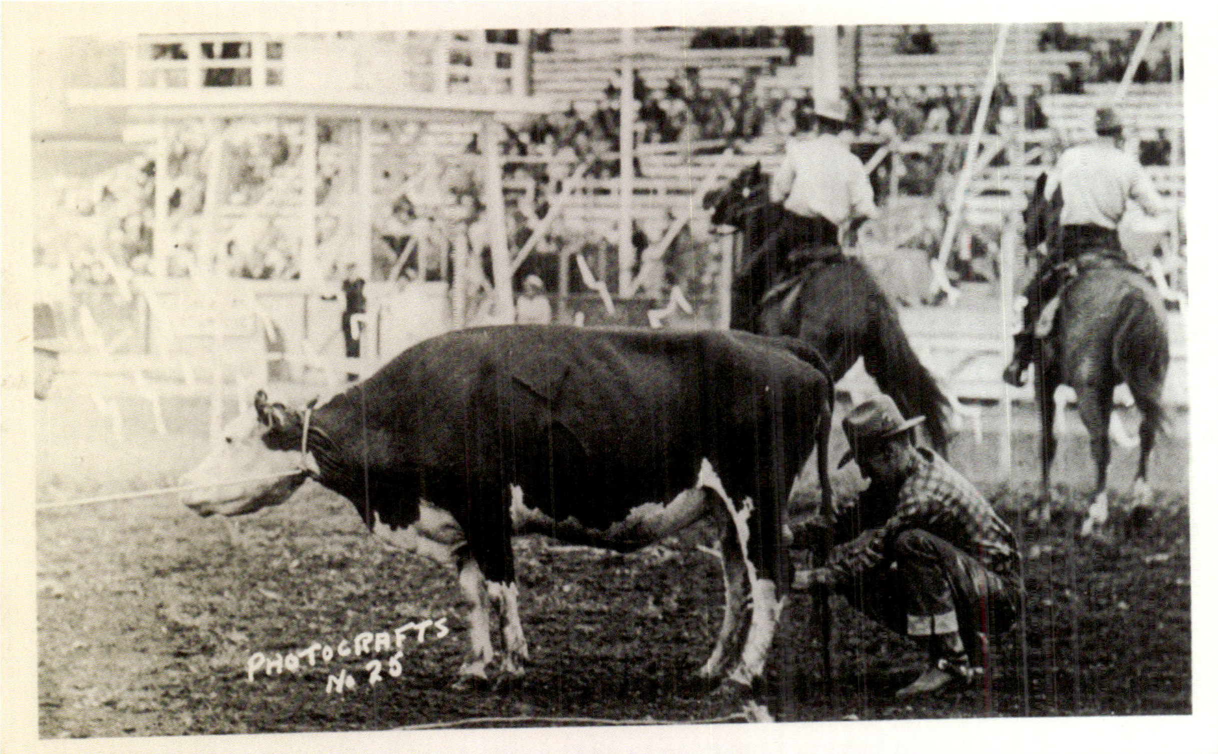

Wild-cow milking, Calgary Stampede

PRAIRIE POSTCARDS PC006198

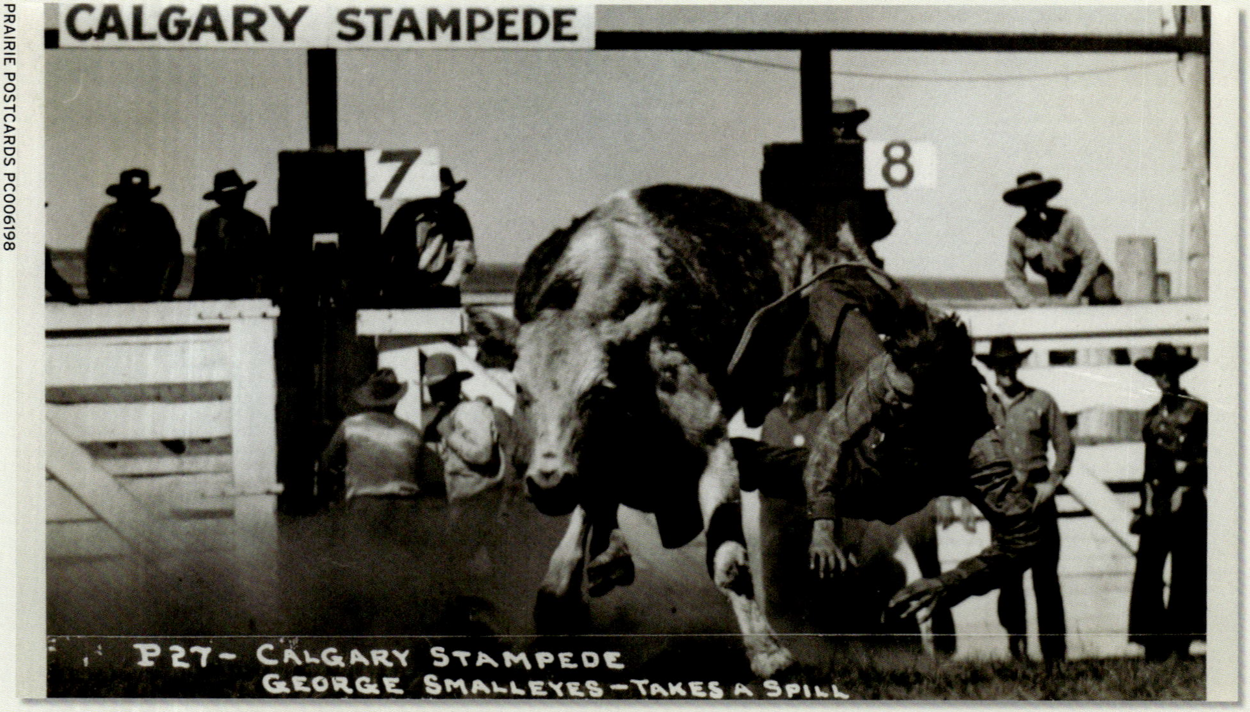

George Smalleyes is seen here taking a tumble during the bull riding event. He was part of the Smalleyes family of Morley that competed frequently at the Stampede over the years. Calgary Photo Supply Co. published this gripping postcard.

PRAIRIE POSTCARDS PC006184

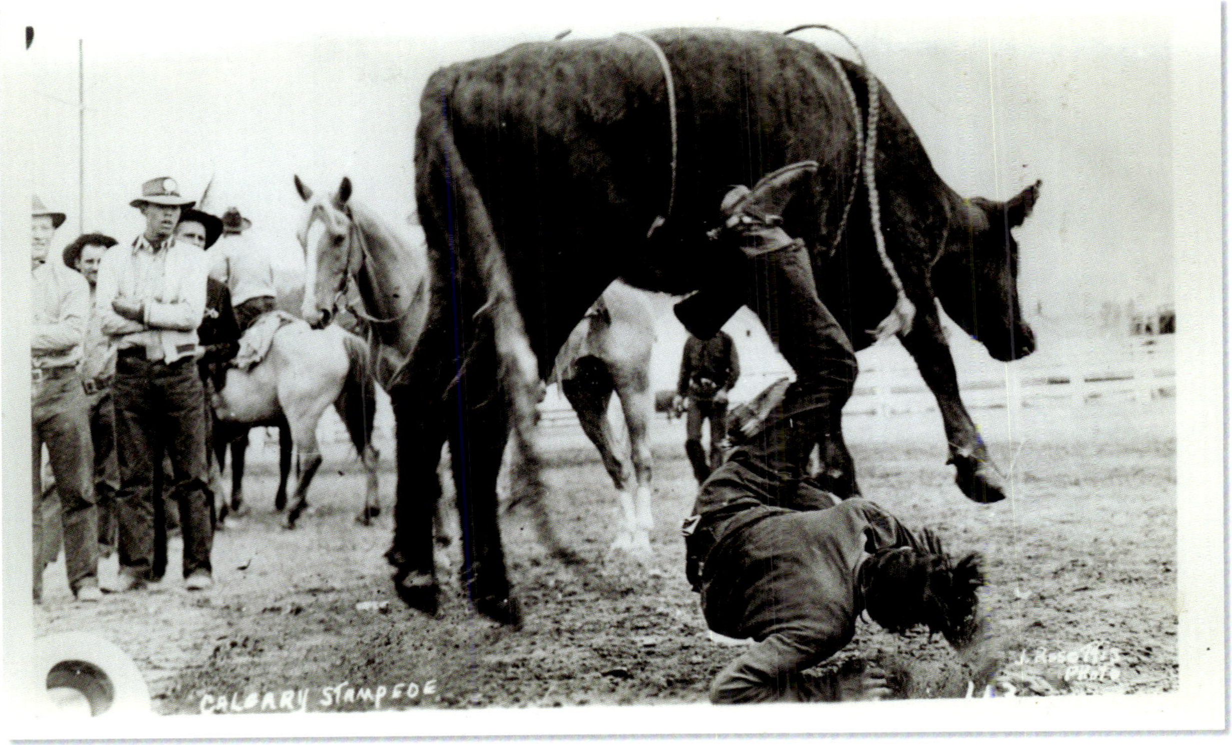

Joe Rosettis catches that bone-crunching moment when a cowboy bites the dust during the steer riding event. Onlooking cowboys, and even the horses, seem to exude a certain empathy.

PRAIRIE POSTCARDS PC006199

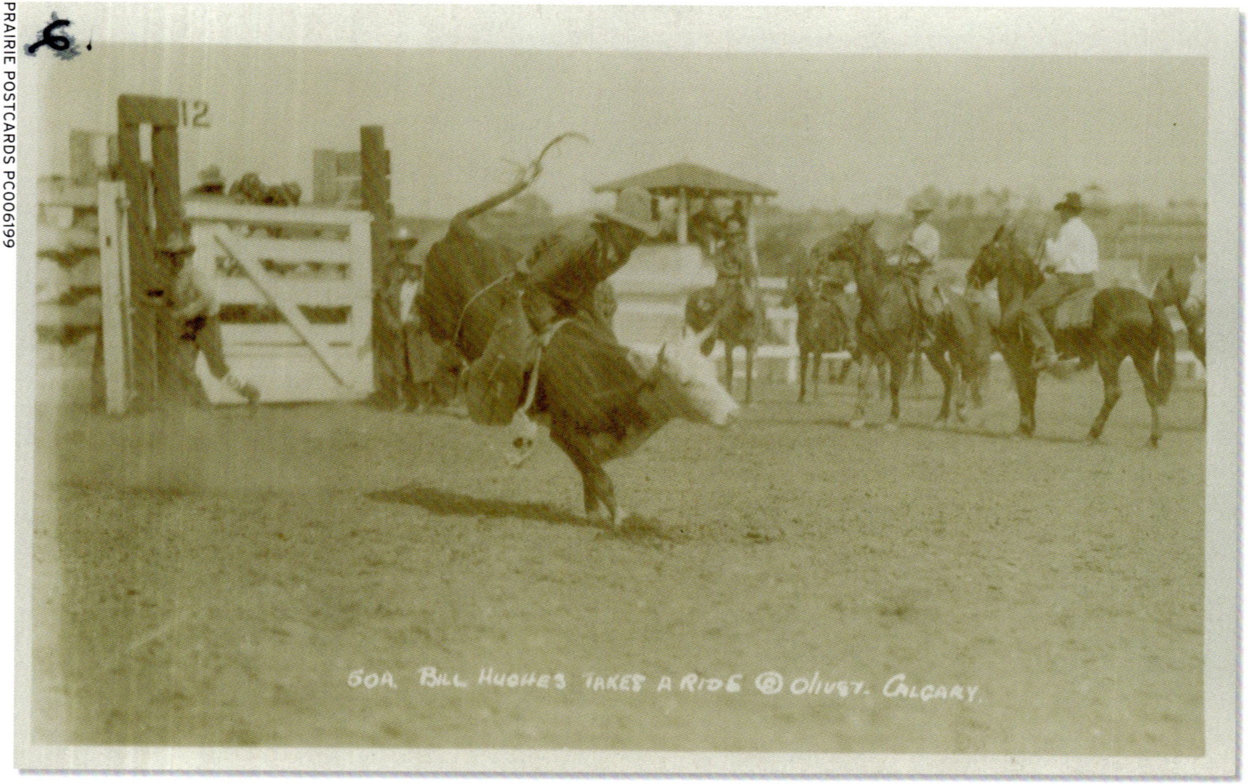

A W.J. Oliver postcard of Bill Hughes as he "takes a ride" during the bull and steer event at the 1929 Stampede

PC016483

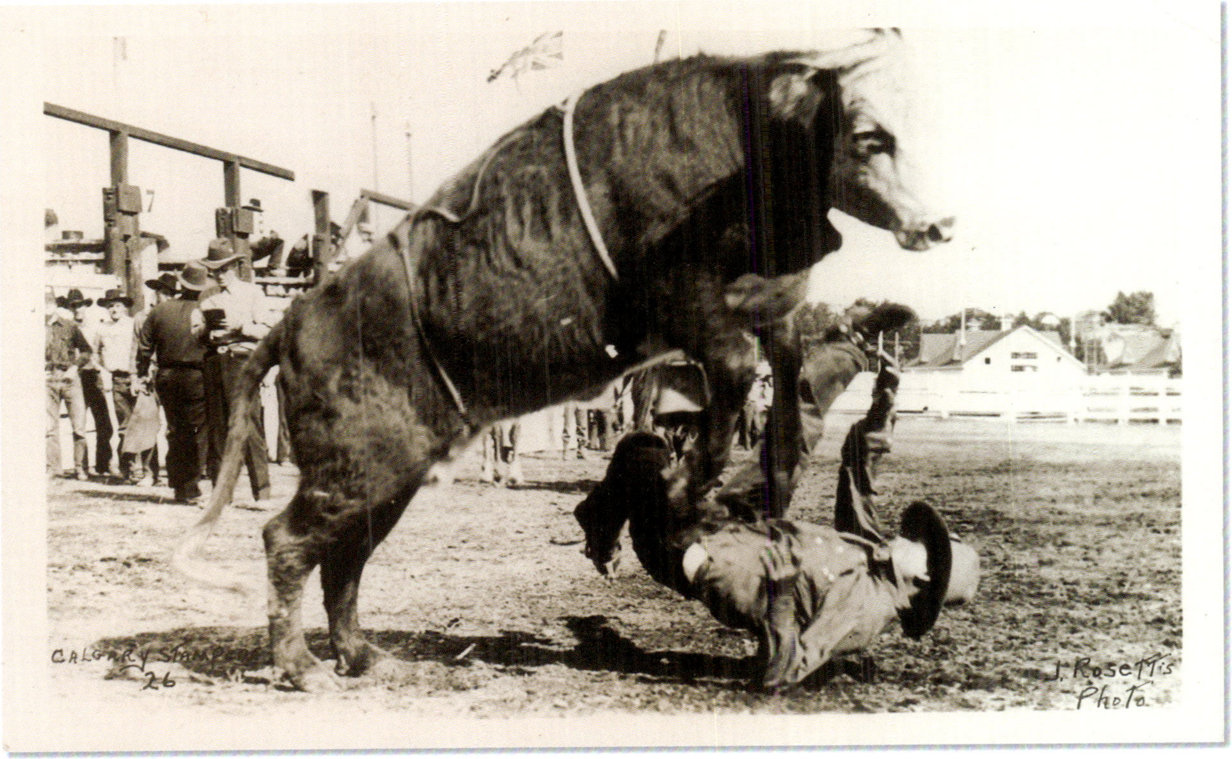

Cowboy thrown from bull at Calgary Stampede

PC018804

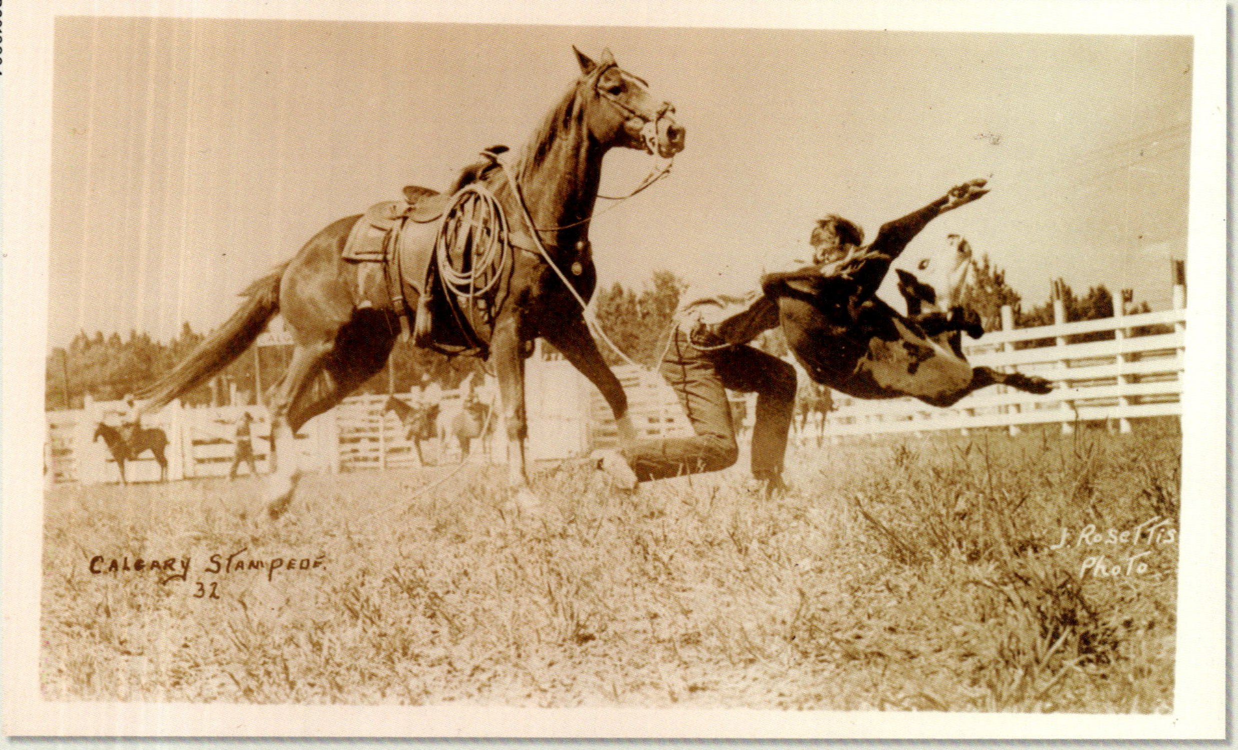

Calf roping

Albert Galarneau, one of the most successful calf ropers, is shown competing in the sport at the Calgary Stampede. The postcard was published by the Calgary Photo Supply Co. Galarneau, a Hanna cowboy, was the last surviving member of the original Cowboys Protective Association (later the Canadian Professional Rodeo Association) board of directors, to which he was elected as calf roping director in 1945. He first entered the boys steer riding event at the Calgary Stampede in 1931, but in 1932 focused on calf roping, for which he became the most famous. In 1937 he won the North American calf roping championship at the Calgary Stampede on his horse Ireland. The following year, he took first in the Canadian calf roping event and second in the North American event. In 1945 Galarneau won the Saskatchewan circuit calf roping championship, and the next year a Charlie Beil bronze statue. He became the first owner of the Calgary Stampede Ranch in 1941 and was inducted into the Canadian Professional Rodeo Hall of Fame in 1986.

PRAIRIE POSTCARDS PC006304

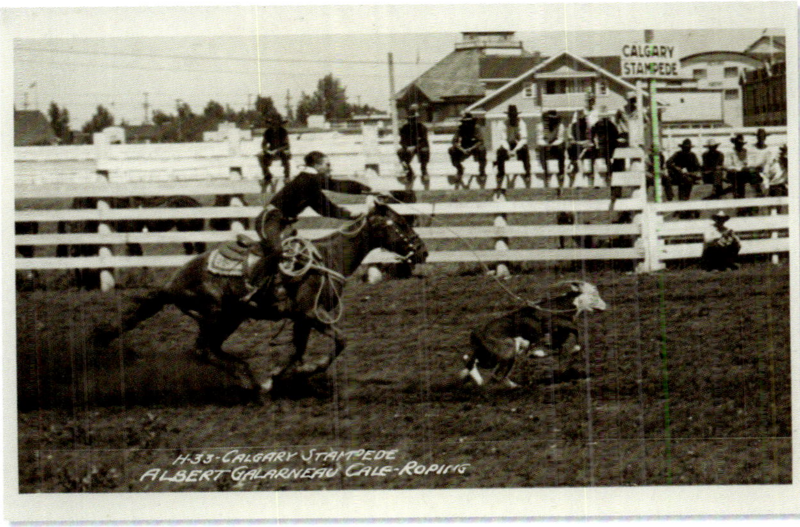

PRAIRIE POSTCARDS PC006309

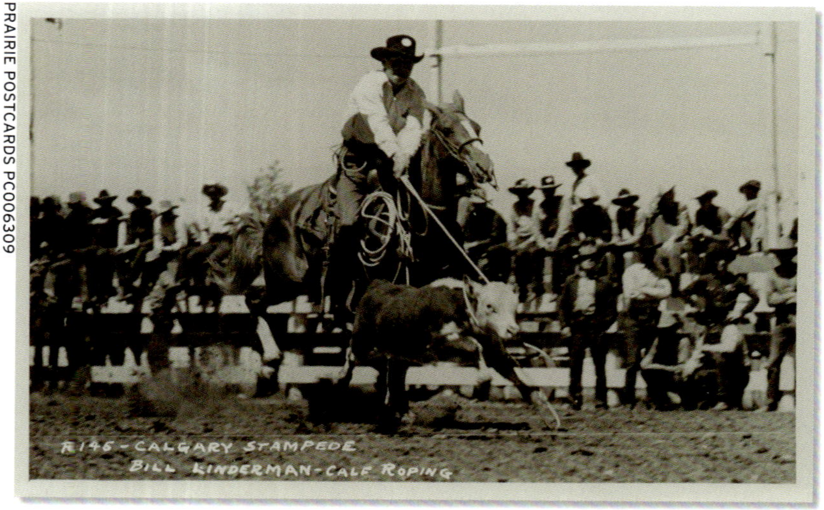

The great Bill Linderman of Red Lodge, Montana, shows his style in the calf roping event at the Calgary Stampede. Calgary Photo Supply Co. made this card as one of many it produced to support the Stampede. Having won the all-around championship at the Calgary Stampede two years before, Linderman became, in 1950, the first man in professional rodeo history to win three world titles in a single season, claiming the championships in the all-around, the steer wrestling and the saddle bronc events. Overall, he won six world championships: All-Around, 1950, 1953; Bareback Riding, 1943; Steer Wrestling, 1950; and Saddle Bronc Riding, 1945, 1950. Linderman died in a plane crash on November 11, 1965, in Salt Lake City.

PRAIRIE POSTCARDS PC006316

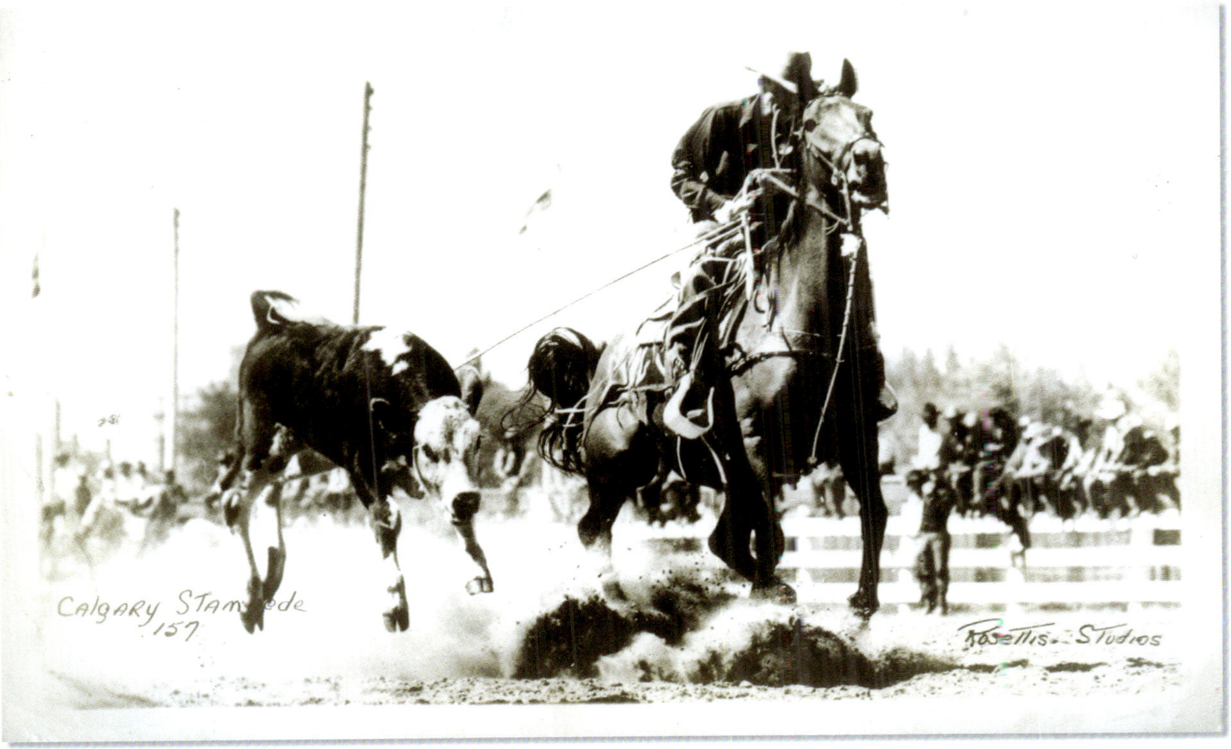

Another great Rosettis postcard view freezes the instant when a cowboy drops his loop on a calf that is seemingly suspended in midair.

PRAIRIE POSTCARDS PC006303

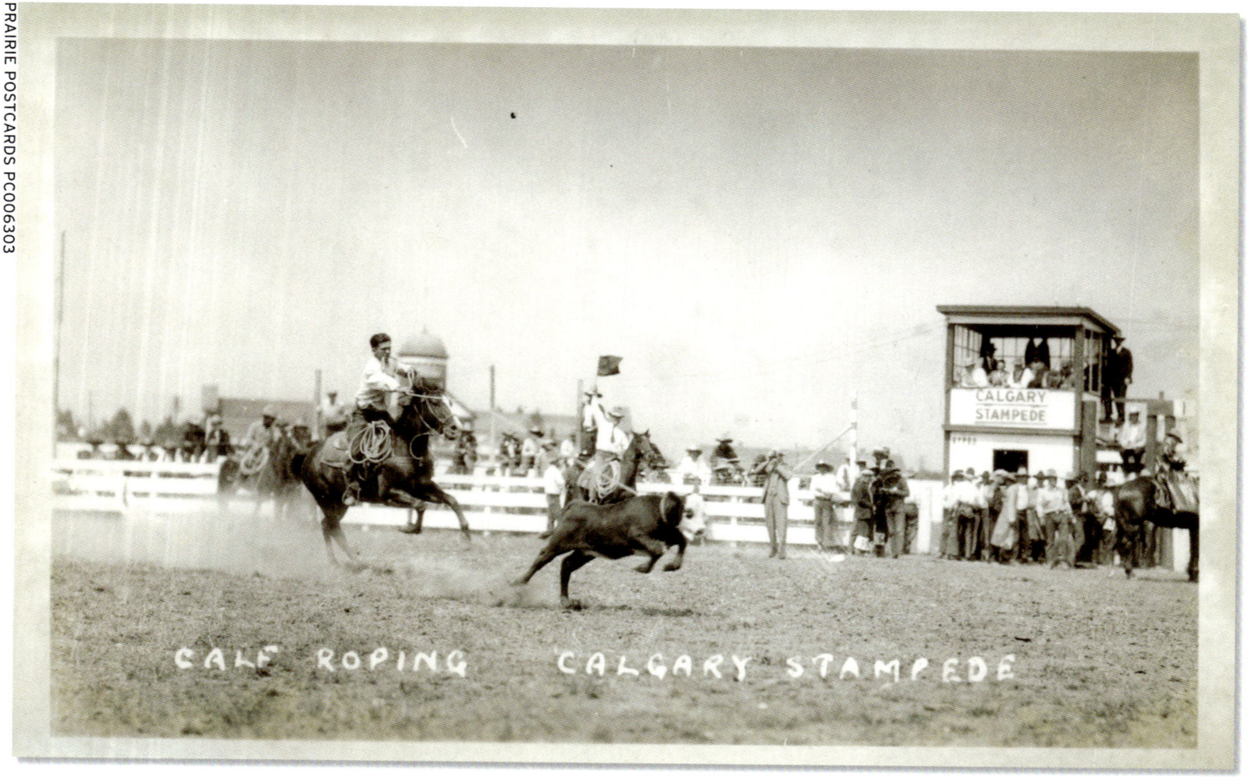

Calf roping was another event introduced in 1912 that remained a perennial crowd pleaser.

PRAIRIE POSTCARDS PC006307

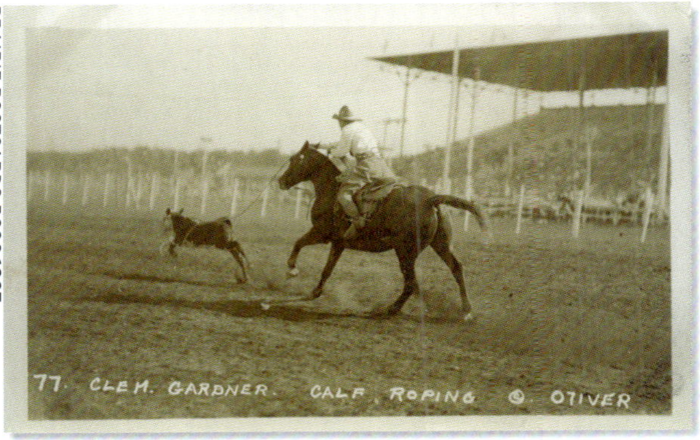

W.J. Oliver captured this image of Clem Gardner in the calf roping event just after the First World War. Gardner had arrived at the Elbow River near Calgary in 1886 when his family came from Manitoba in a covered wagon driving a hundred head of cattle. Clem grew up on the ranch and honed his skills to the point where he was named the first All-Round Cowboy at the inaugural Calgary Stampede in 1912. He kept his connection with the Stampede and in 1931 ran the champion chuckwagon outfit. He became a highly respected horse show judge and competitor and was also a competition polo player. Gardner served as president of the Alberta Thoroughbred Association and the Alberta Horse Breeders Association. He died in 1963 and was posthumously inducted into the Canadian Professional Rodeo Hall of Fame in 1985.

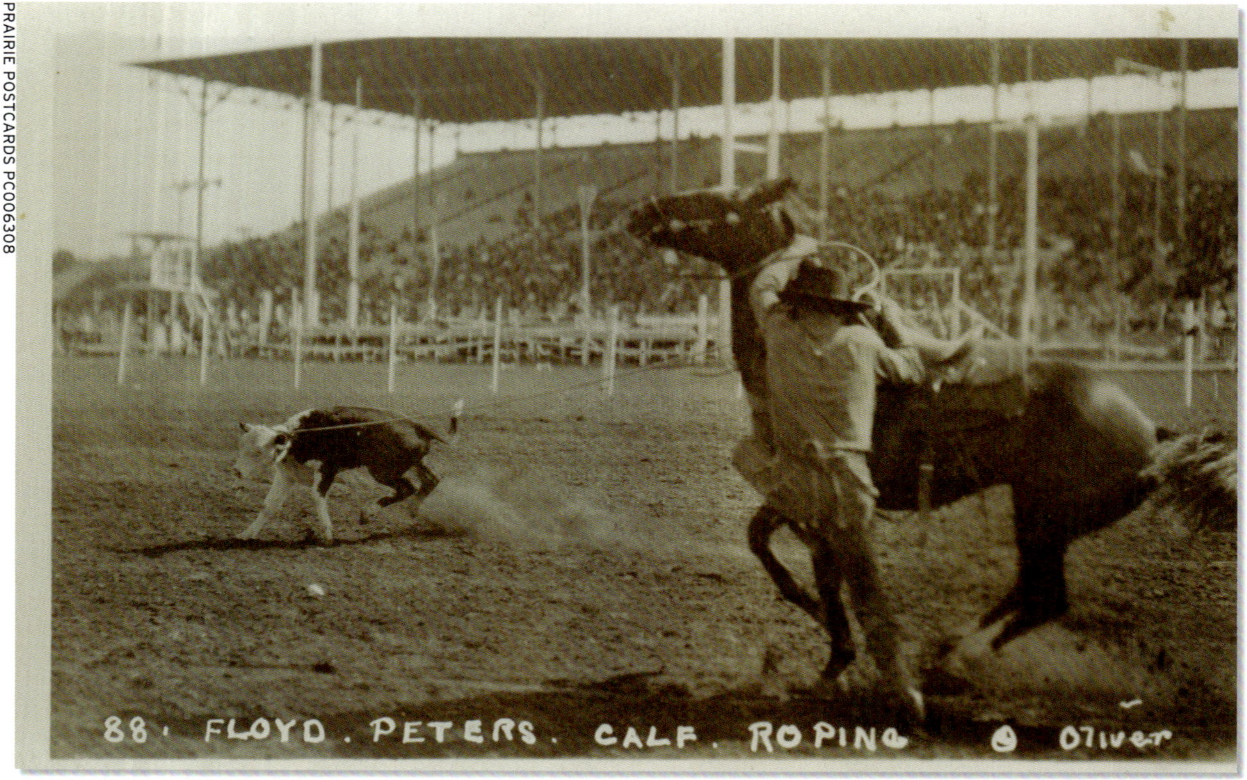

Floyd Peters, from Cardston, Alberta, in the calf roping competition about 1930. Photographed by W.J. Oliver.

Even before the Calgary Exhibition & Stampede was established, Toronto publishers Warwick Bros. & Rutter Ltd. saw the value of marketing the Western Canadian image of the valiant cowboy riding a bucking bronco. This card seems to date from about 1907.

PRAIRIE POSTCARDS PC009868

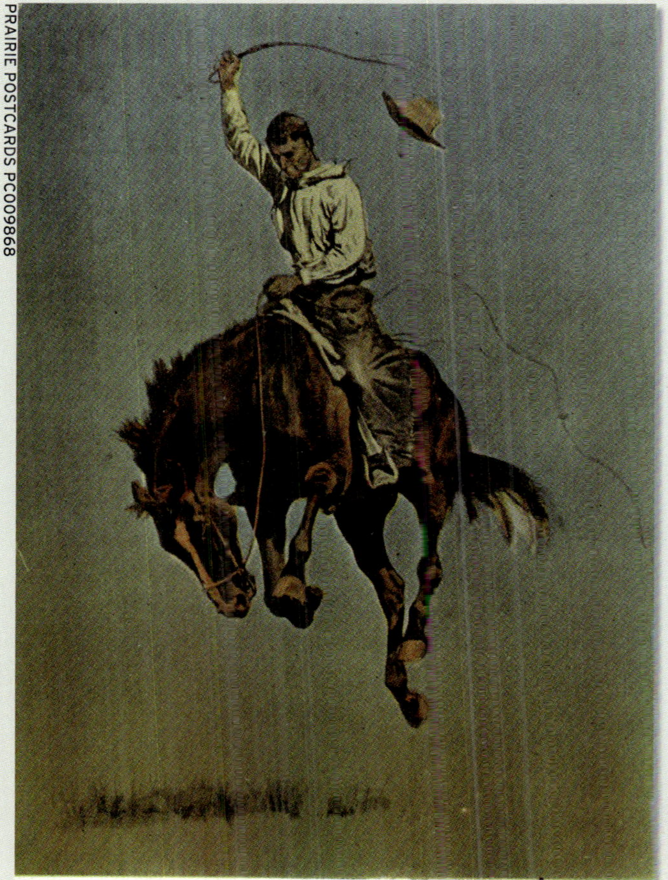

BUCKING BRONCHO WESTERN CANADA

1299

PRAIRIE POSTCARDS PC006274

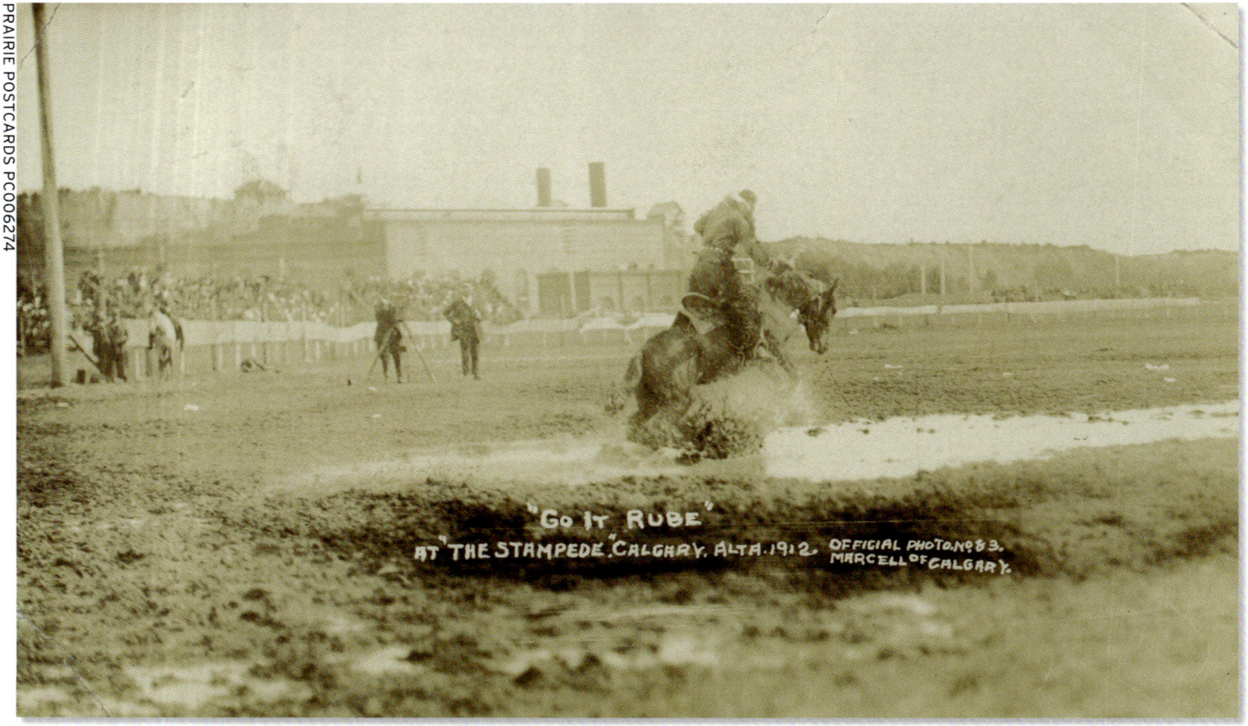

"Go it, Rube," another classic Marcell of Calgary image from the first Stampede, 1912

PRAIRIE POSTCARDS PC006269

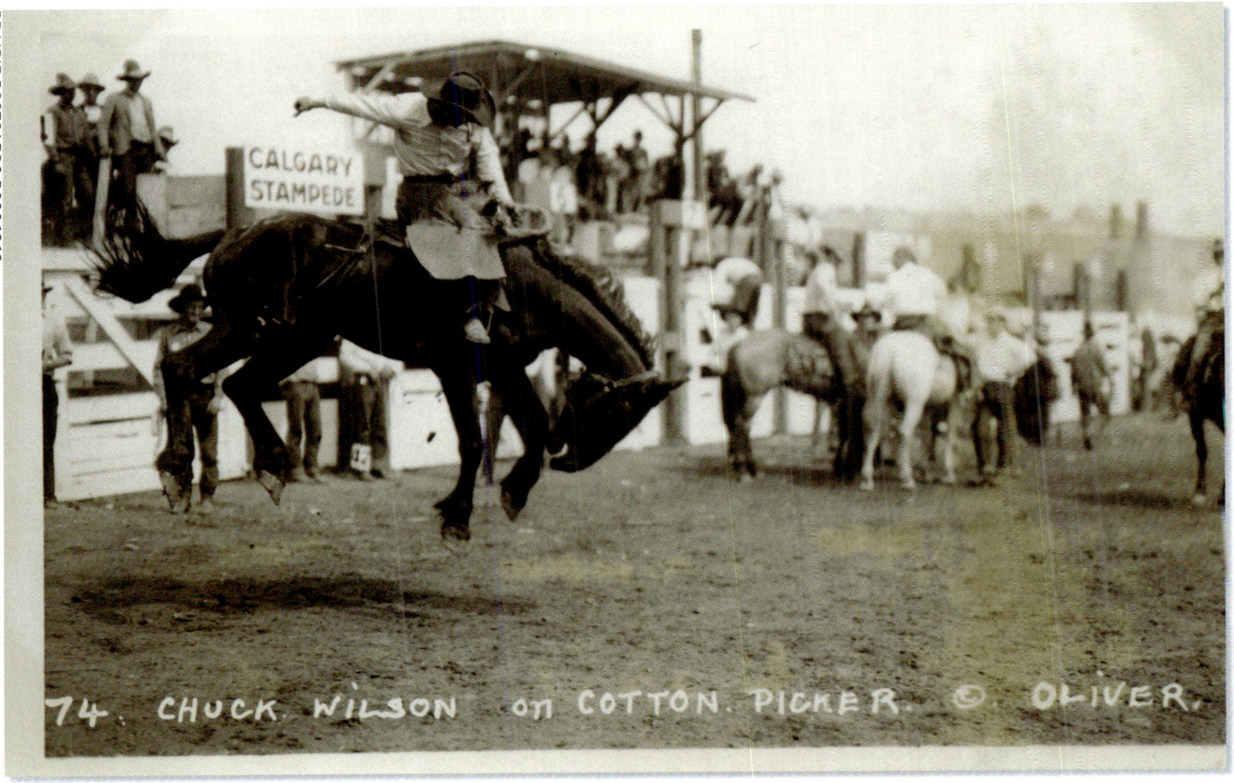

Chuck Wilson riding Cotton Picker on July 11, 1930. Another great W.J. Oliver action postcard.

PRAIRIE POSTCARDS PC012034

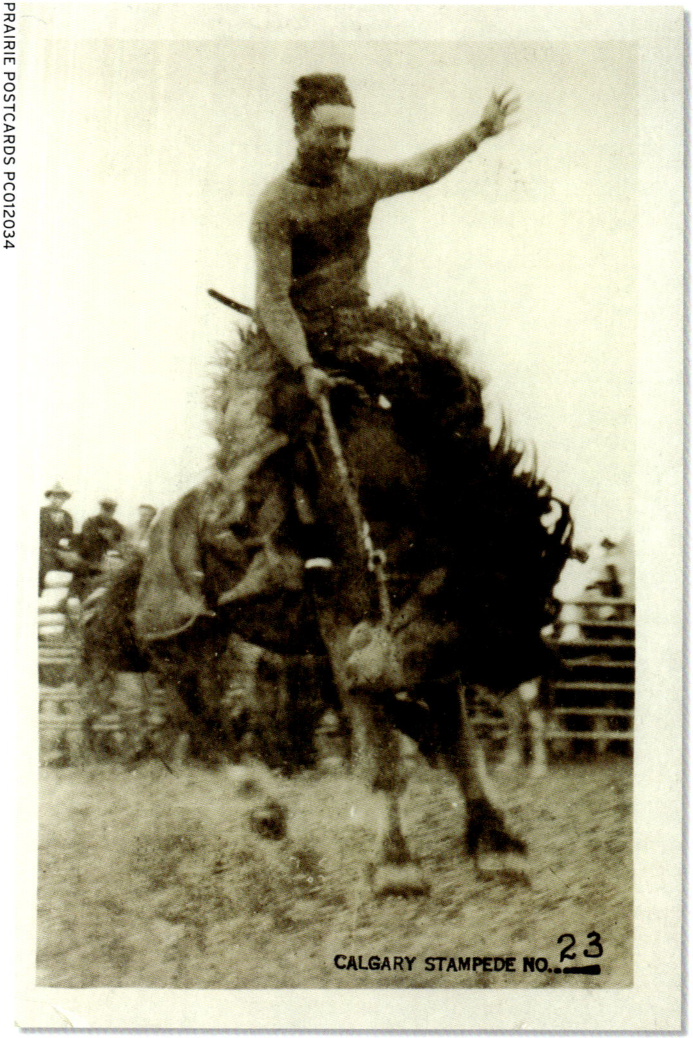

Saddle bronc riding at the 1924 Calgary Stampede

PRAIRIE POSTCARDS PC006293

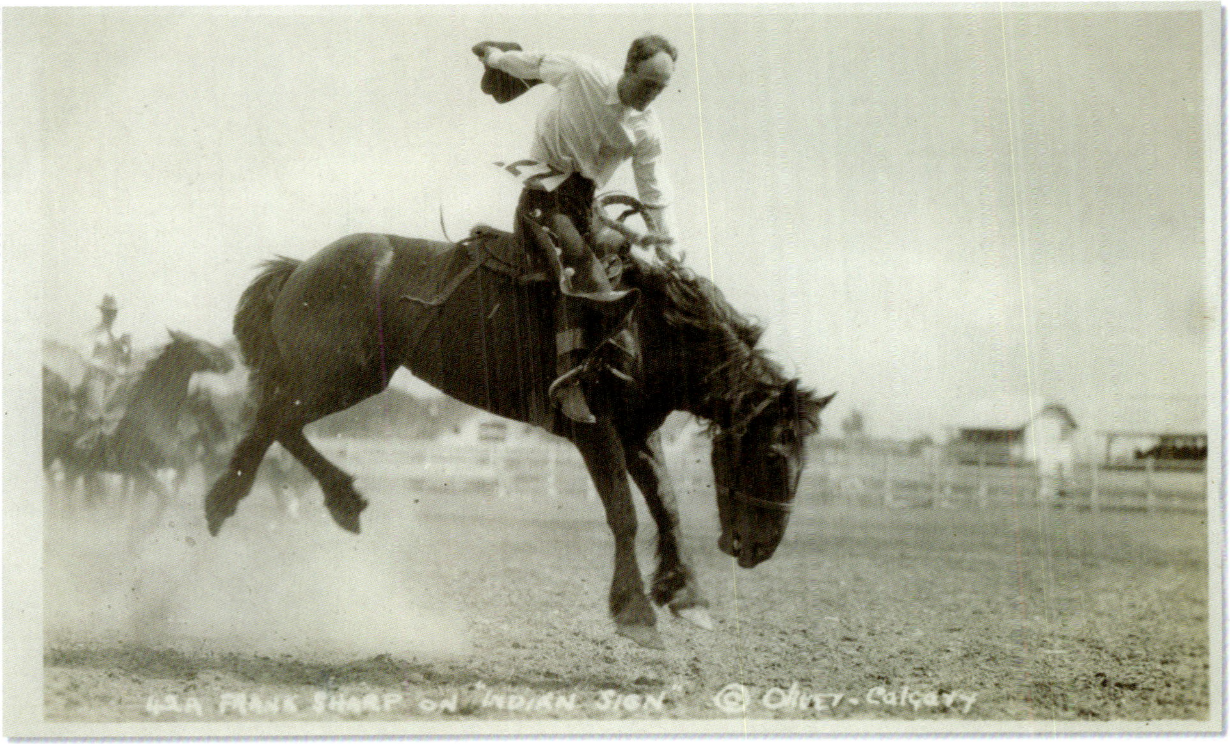

Part of the W.J. Oliver series of Calgary Stampede postcards. In this one, Frank Sharp, a regular contestant during the latter part of the 1920s, rides the saddle bronc Indian Sign at the 1929 Stampede.

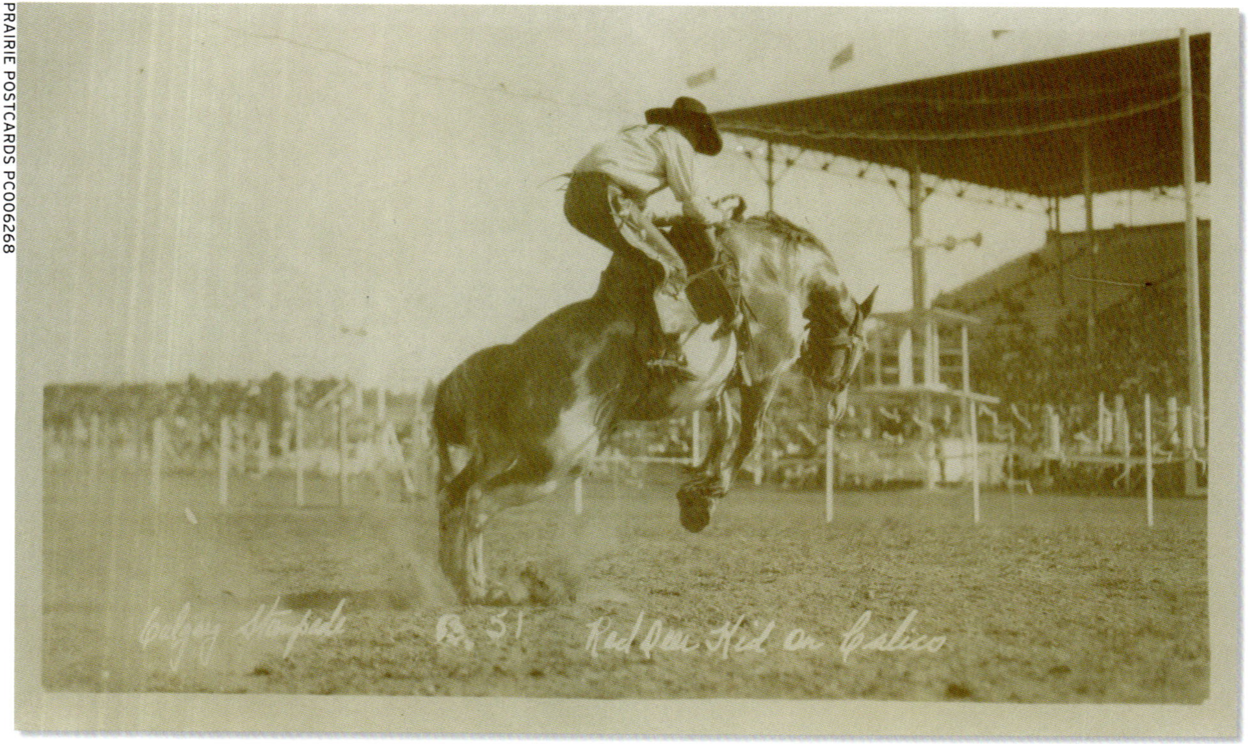

PRAIRIE POSTCARDS PC006268

The Red Deer Kid rides Calico in about 1930, in another of the McDermid Photo Laboratories series of Stampede postcards. Calico was a famous bucking horse during the late 1920s and early 1930s.

PRAIRIE POSTCARDS PC006282

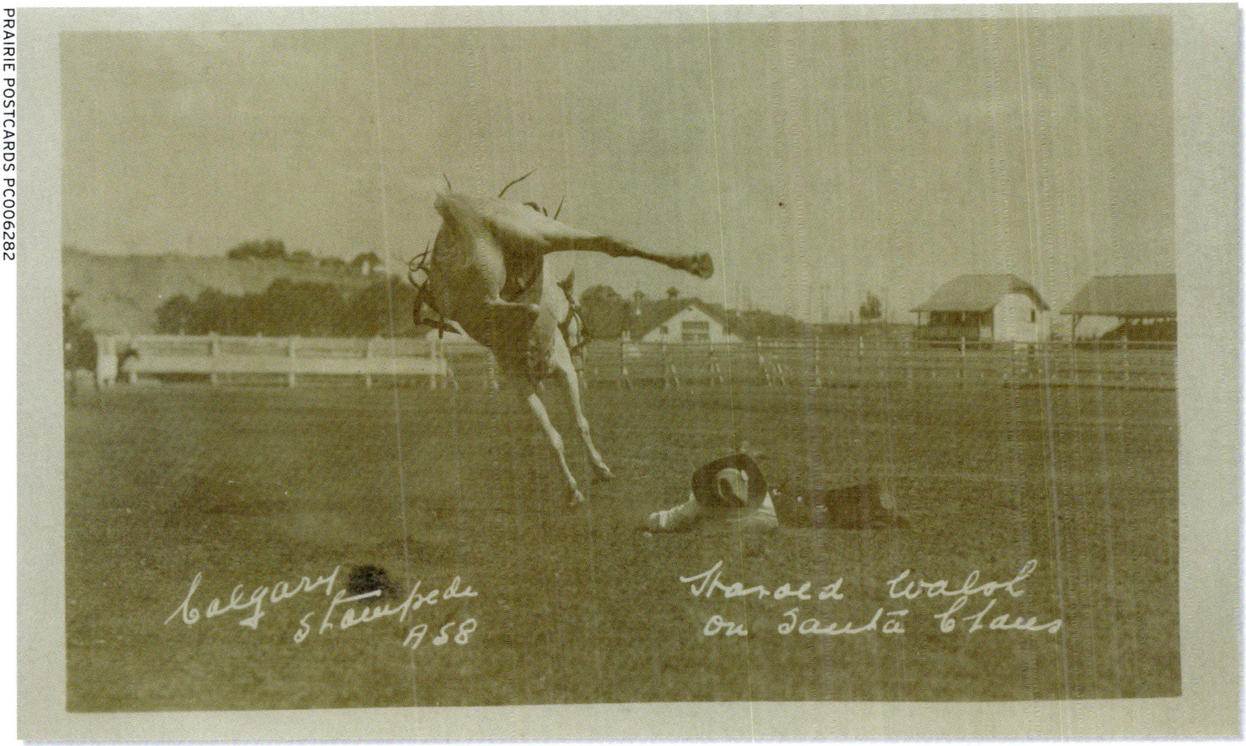

Harold Walsh gets thrown by Santa Claus at the 1929 Calgary Stampede, caught for posterity by McDermid Photo Laboratories.

PRAIRIE POSTCARDS PC006278

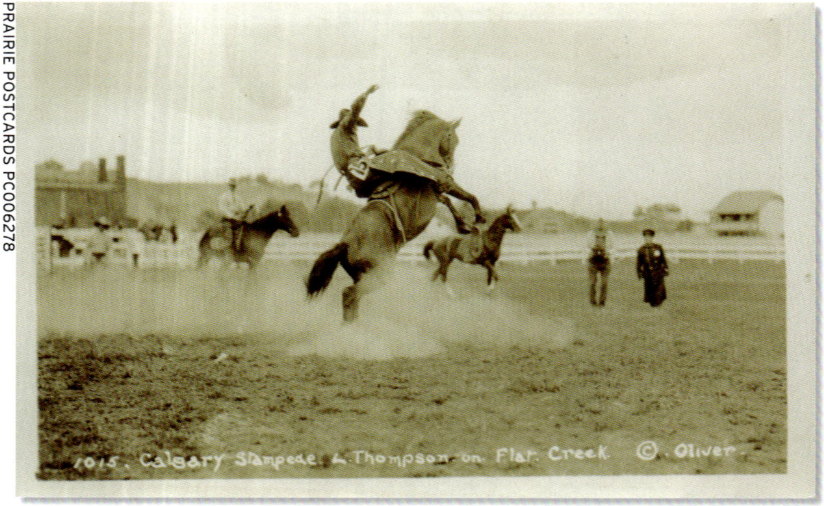

The famous photographer W.J. Oliver captured Lorne Thompson riding Flat Creek at the 1927 Stampede. Recognized as one of the top bronc riders in the Canadian West in the 1920s and 1930s, Thompson was one of the organizers of the Medicine Hat Exhibition & Stampede Company in 1947 and later served as president. He also was a Medicine Hat alderman for a number of years. The Cypress Centre facility on the 'Hat Stampede grounds was dedicated in honour of this fine gentleman and builder of the rodeo sport, and Thompson was inducted into the Sports Hall of Fame in his home city in 1983.

PRAIRIE POSTCARDS PC006283

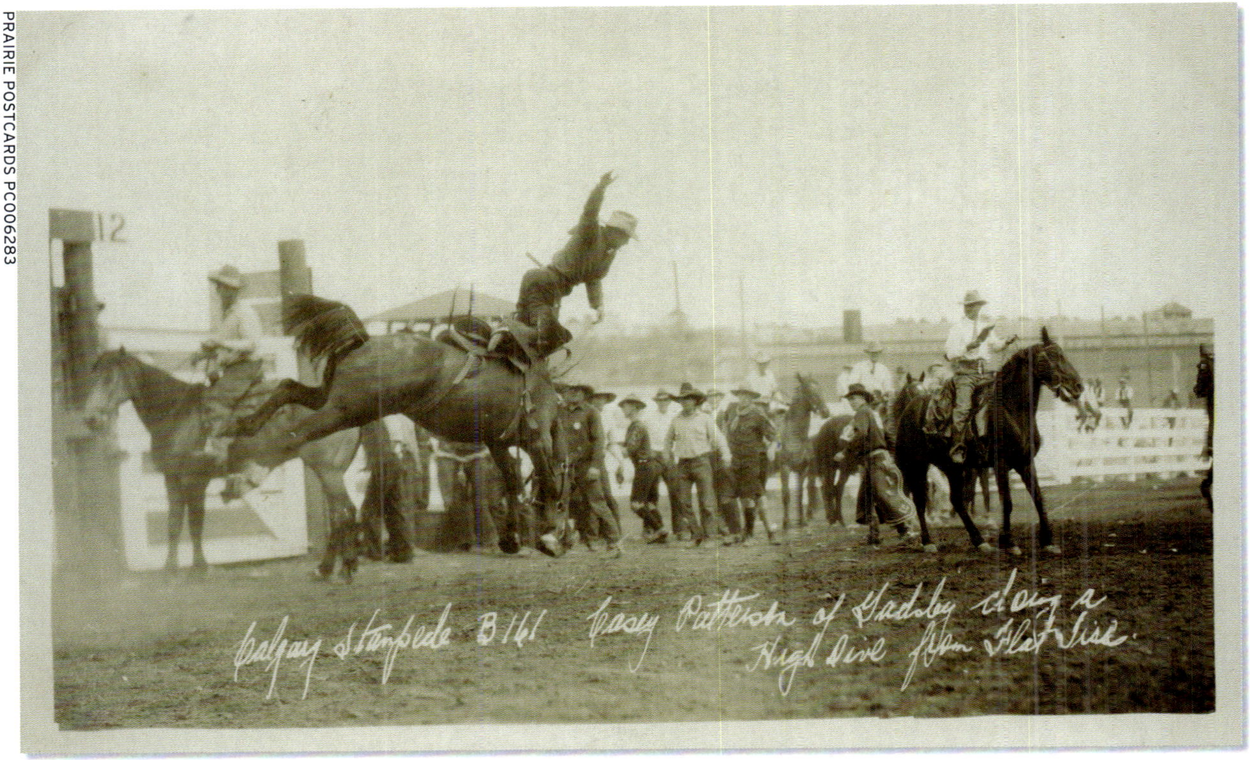

Casey Patterson, from Gadsby, Alberta, takes his leave of Flat Tire at the 1930 Calgary Stampede.

PRAIRIE POSTCARDS PC006267

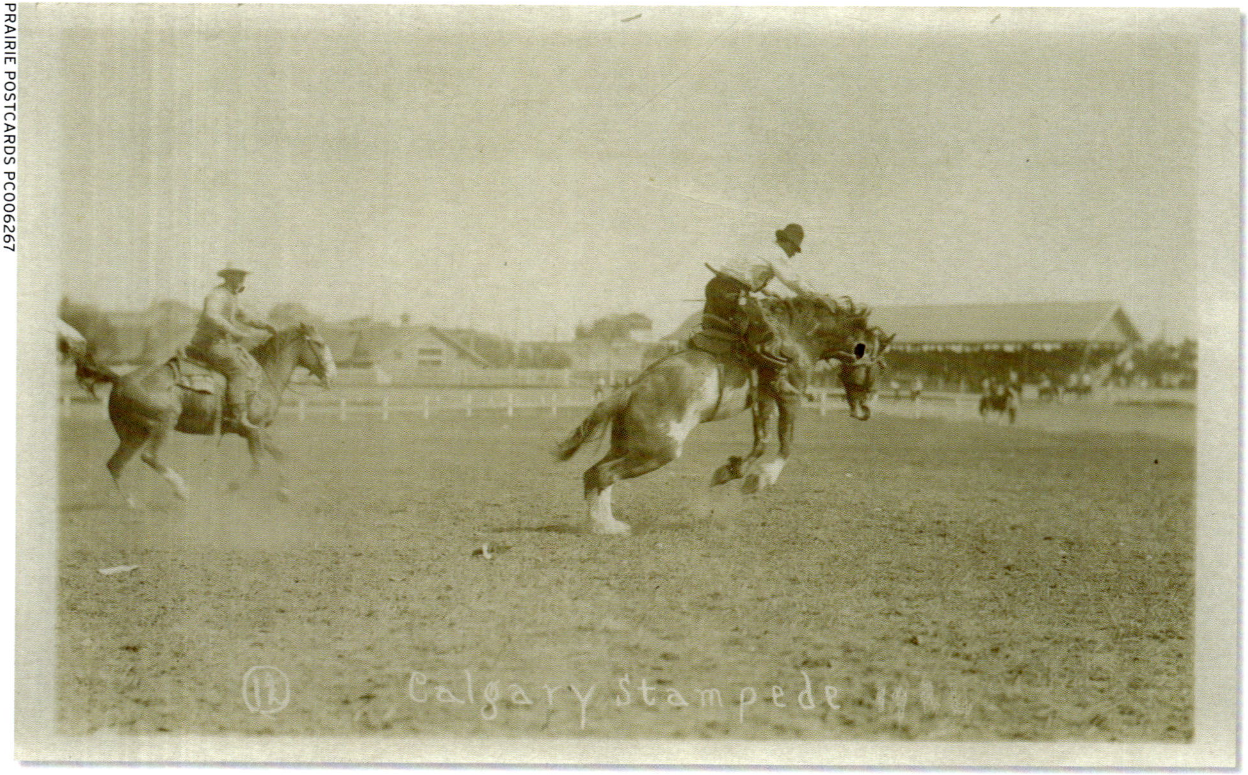

Hard-riding action during the saddle bronc event at the 1924 Stampede

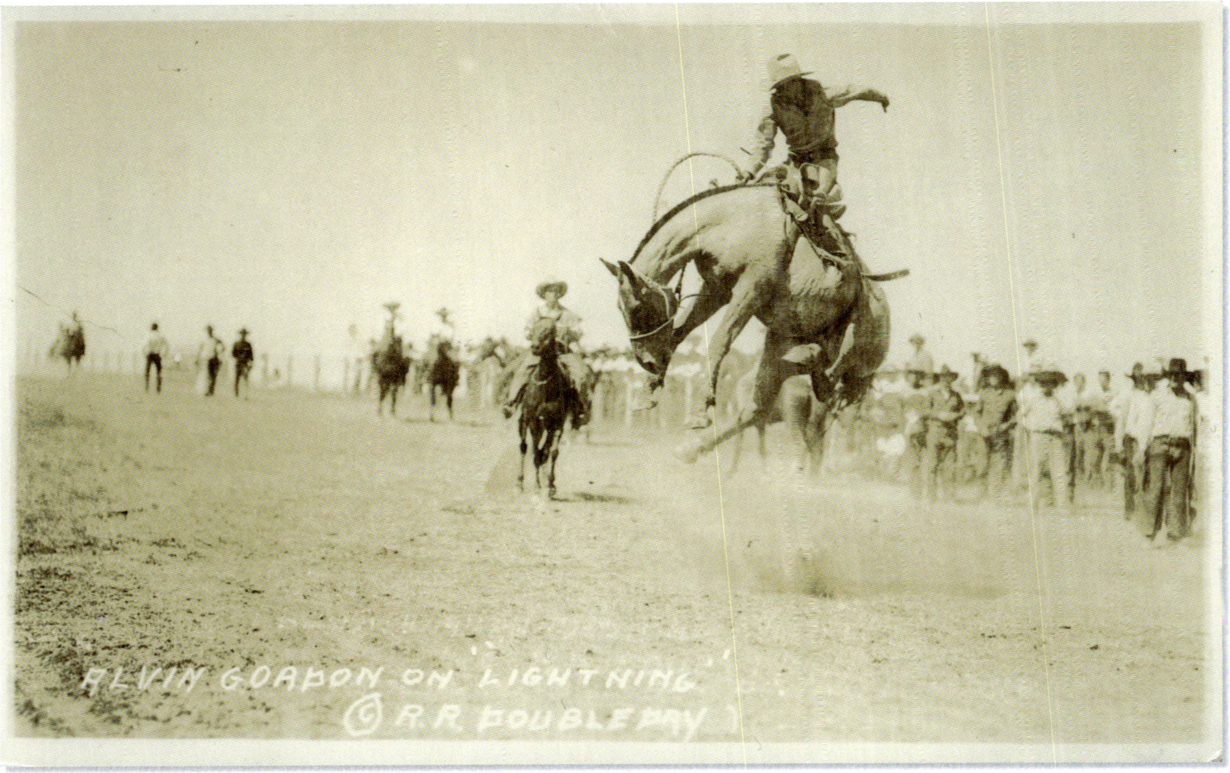

Alvin Gordon riding Lightning in this action-packed shot by R.R. Doubleday

PRAIRIE POSTCARDS PC006257

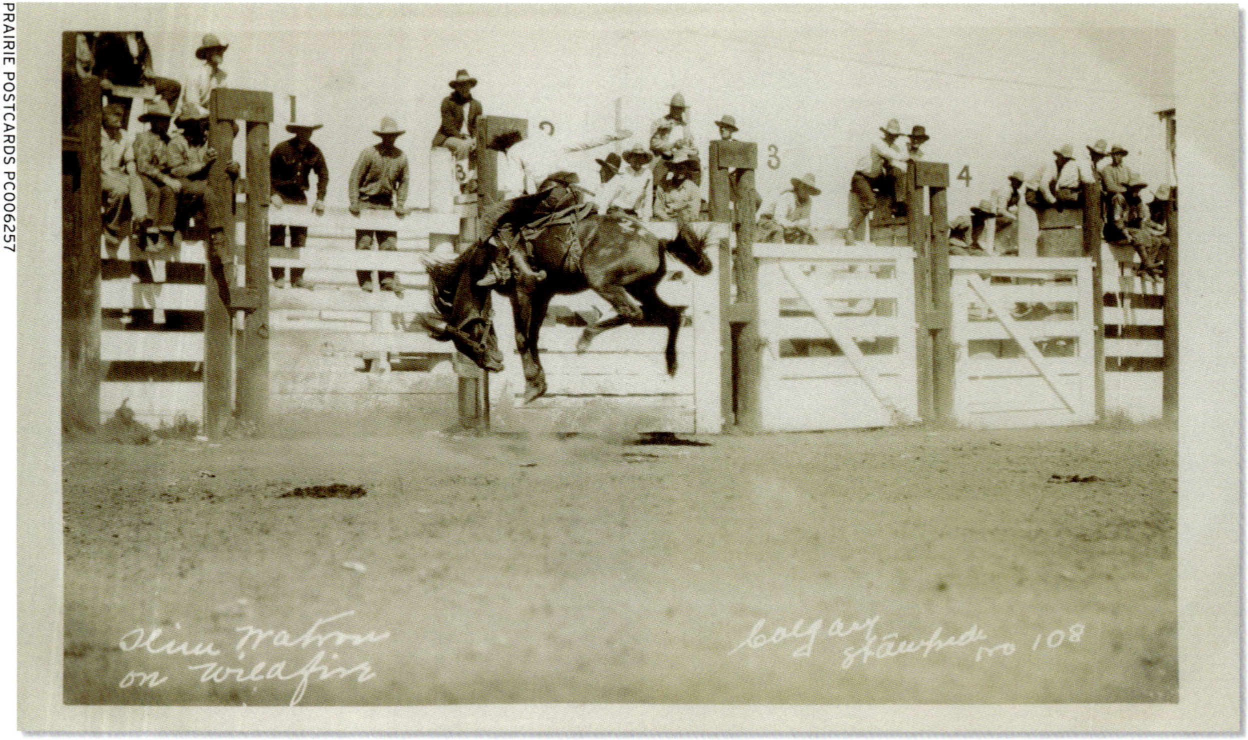

Slim Watrin rides Wildfire in this riveting image published in the 1920s by McDermid Photo Laboratories of Calgary.

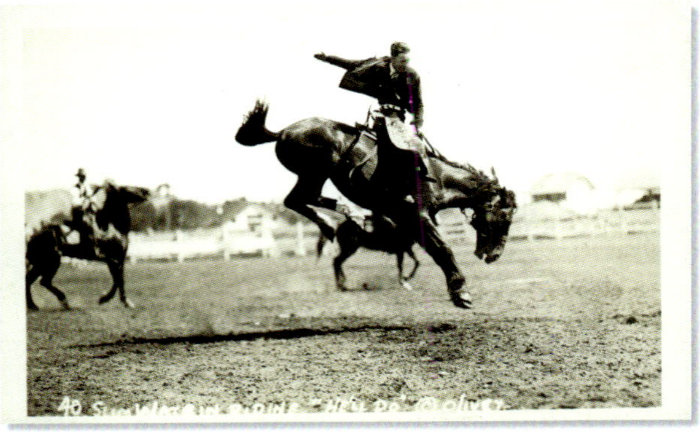

Slim Watrin on He'll Do, at the Calgary Stampede 1931, part of the W.J. Oliver postcard series. Born in Iowa in 1901, Slim Watrin was nine years old when he moved with his family to a ranch in the High River district of Alberta. He took over the ranch when his father died seven years later. Watrin rode in his first saddle bronc competition at Aldersyde, Alberta, and won first prize when he was eighteen. In 1924 he won 13 of the 16 rodeos he entered. Two years later he won the saddle bronc riding at the Ottawa Centenary Rodeo, with a $1,500 prize and the Douglas Fairbanks trophy. At Toronto that same year, he captured the bronc riding again and was awarded the Carls-Rite Hotel trophy. At the 1928 Calgary Stampede, Slim won the North American title with two trophies, one donated by the Chrysler Company, the other by the Governor General of Canada. He also travelled to a rodeo in Chicago that year, where he won money on 12 of the 14 days. Winning the Canadian title at Calgary in 1931, Slim was awarded a white-gold pocket watch, the E.W. Beatty trophy and a silver cigarette case donated by the Prince of Wales.

PRAIRIE POSTCARDS PC006256

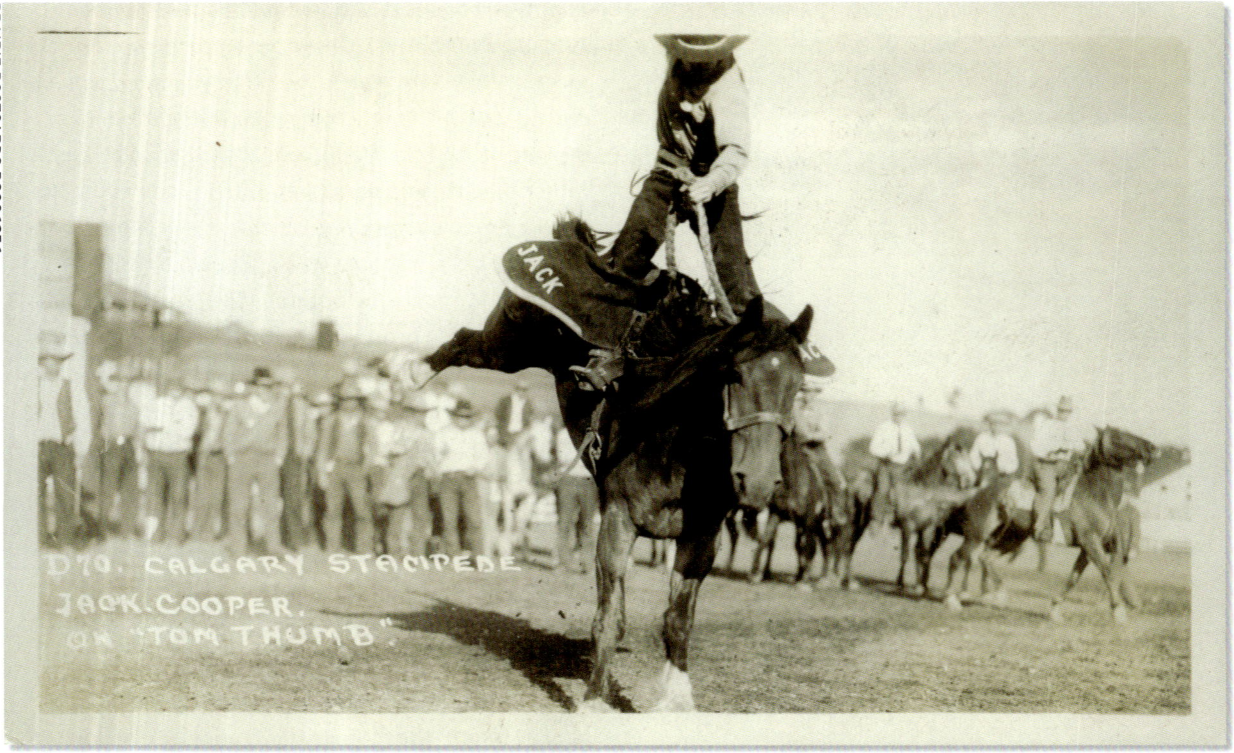

Jack Cooper riding Tom Thumb, published by Calgary Photo Supply Co.

PRAIRIE POSTCARDS PC006249

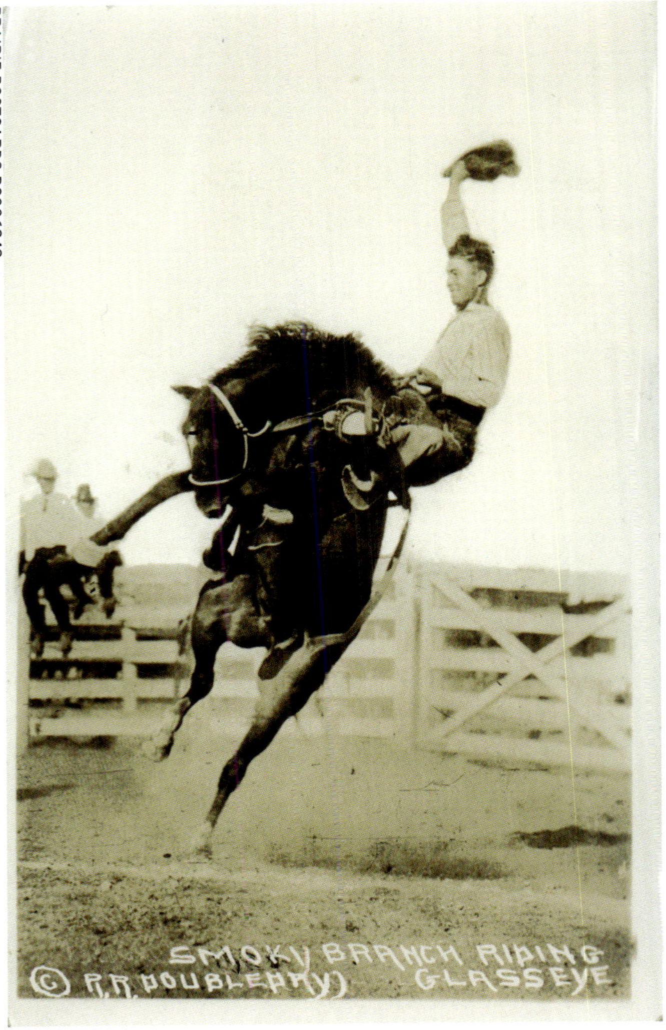

While not from the Calgary Stampede, this is by far one of the best Doubleday images, showing Smoky Branch riding Glass Eye. Over the years, this shot has been given a variety of dates and attributed to numerous locations. It was in fact taken at Garden City, Kansas, in 1921.

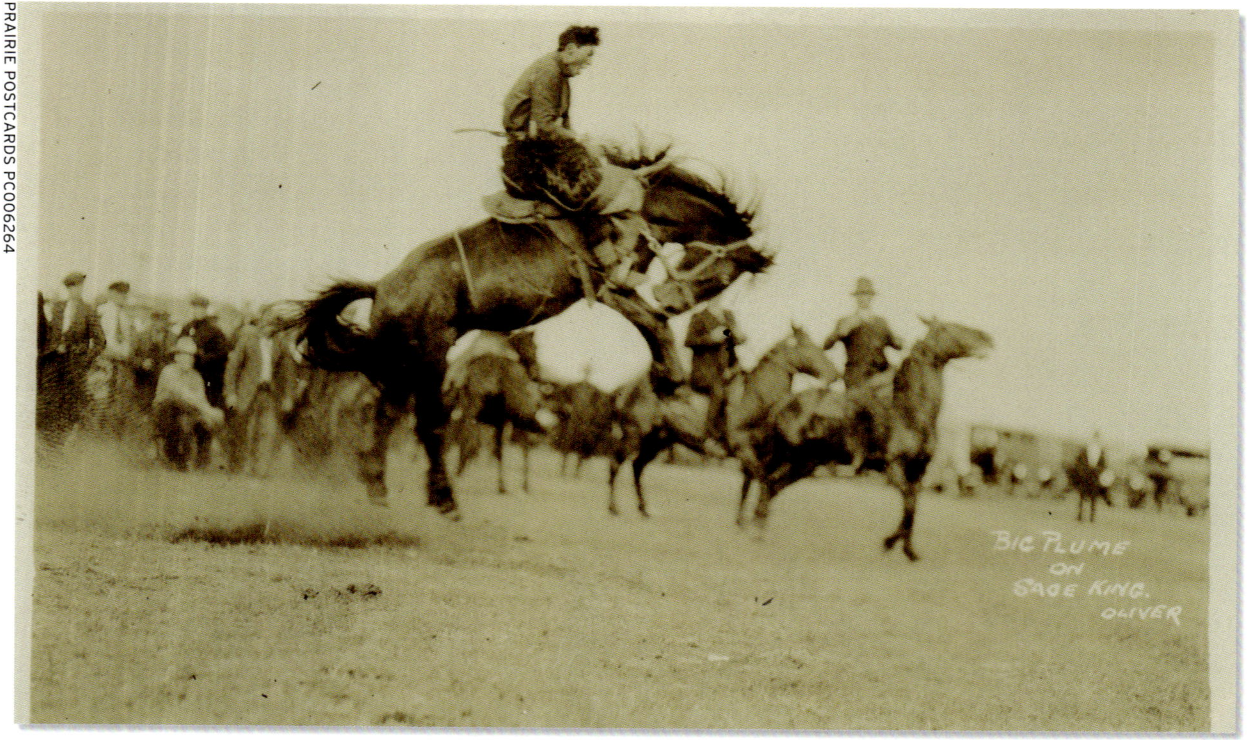

PRAIRIE POSTCARDS PC006264

Big Plume is seen here riding Sage King about 1925.
W.J. Oliver was the photographer.

PRAIRIE POSTCARDS PC006229

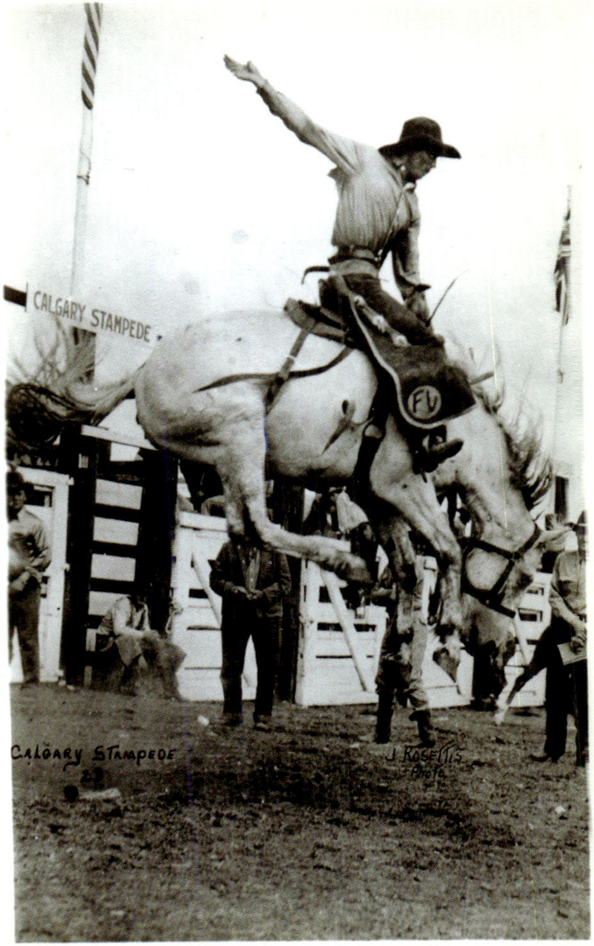

This remains one of the best Joe Rosettis rodeo portraits. A saddle bronc rider is caught in mid-flight, his arm extended in the classic attitude, at the apogee of a sunfishing ride.

PRAIRIE POSTCARDS PC006275

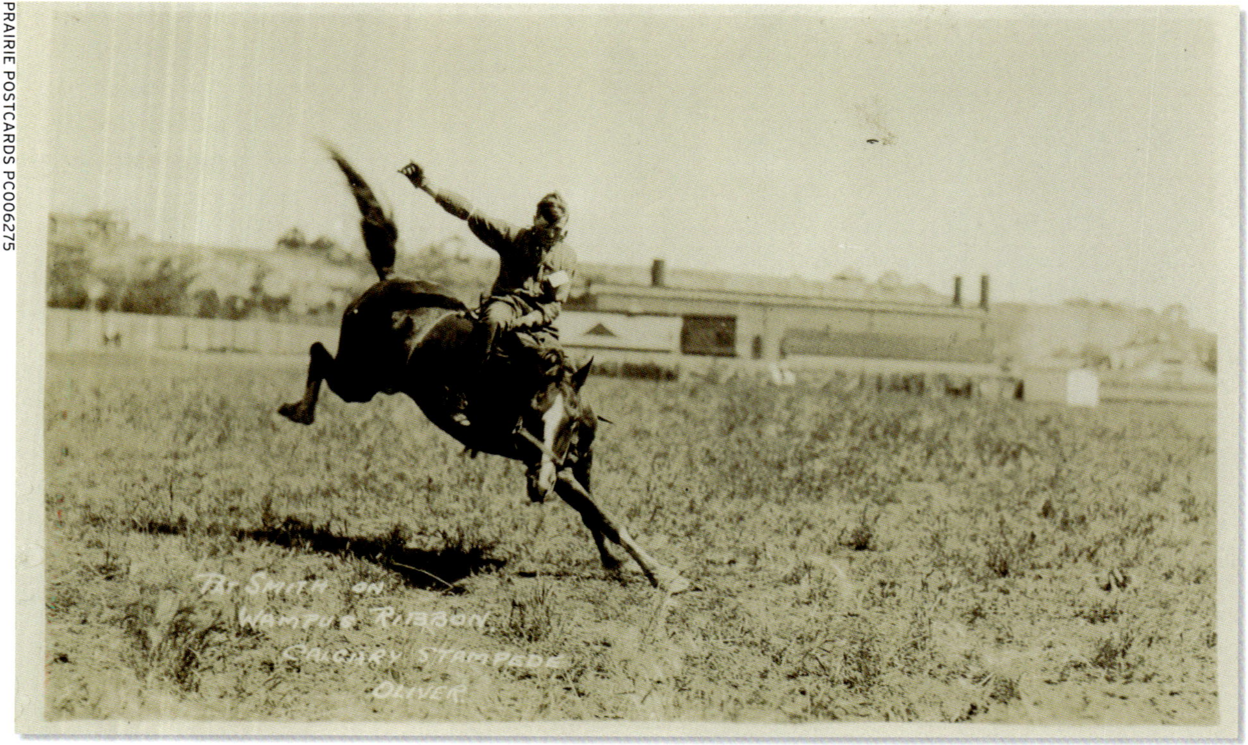

Pat Smith on Wampus Ribbon, bucking across the seemingly endless fields at the Calgary Stampede in the early 1920s. A W.J. Oliver image.

PRAIRIE POSTCARDS PC006286

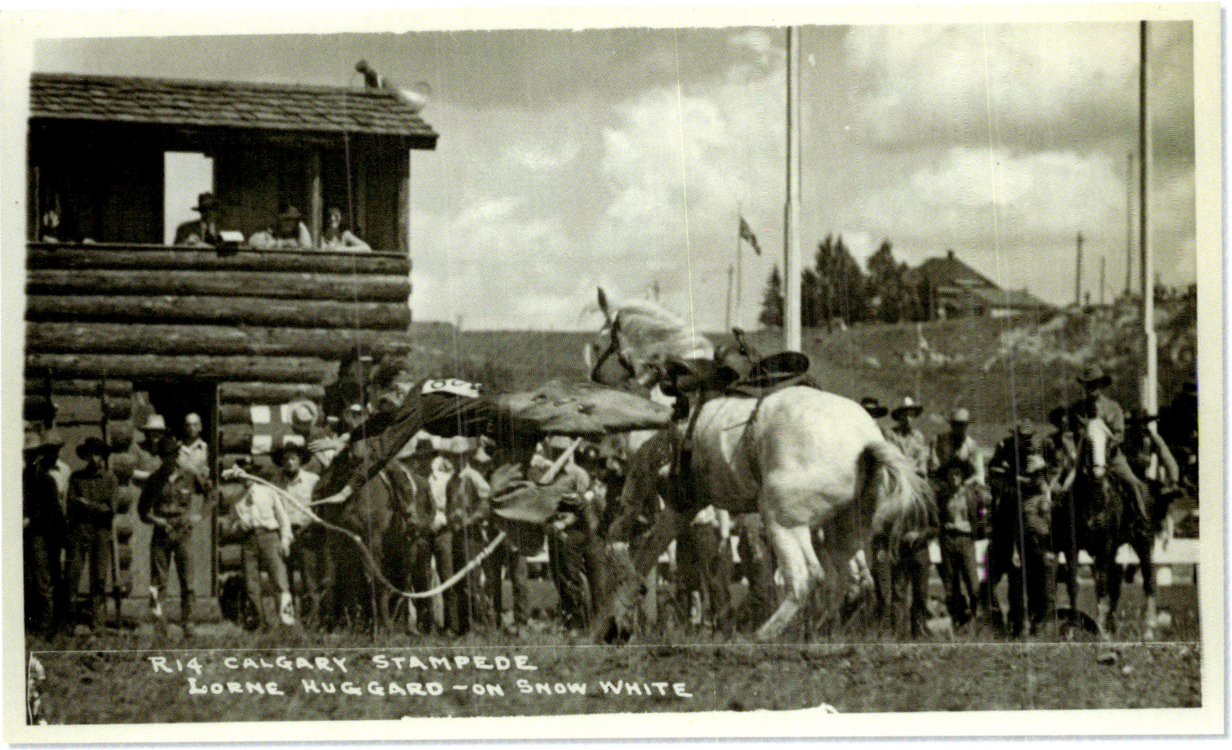

Lorne Huggard flies through the air à la Superman as he departs Snow White on July 10, 1944. Another Calgary Photo Supply Co. postcard.

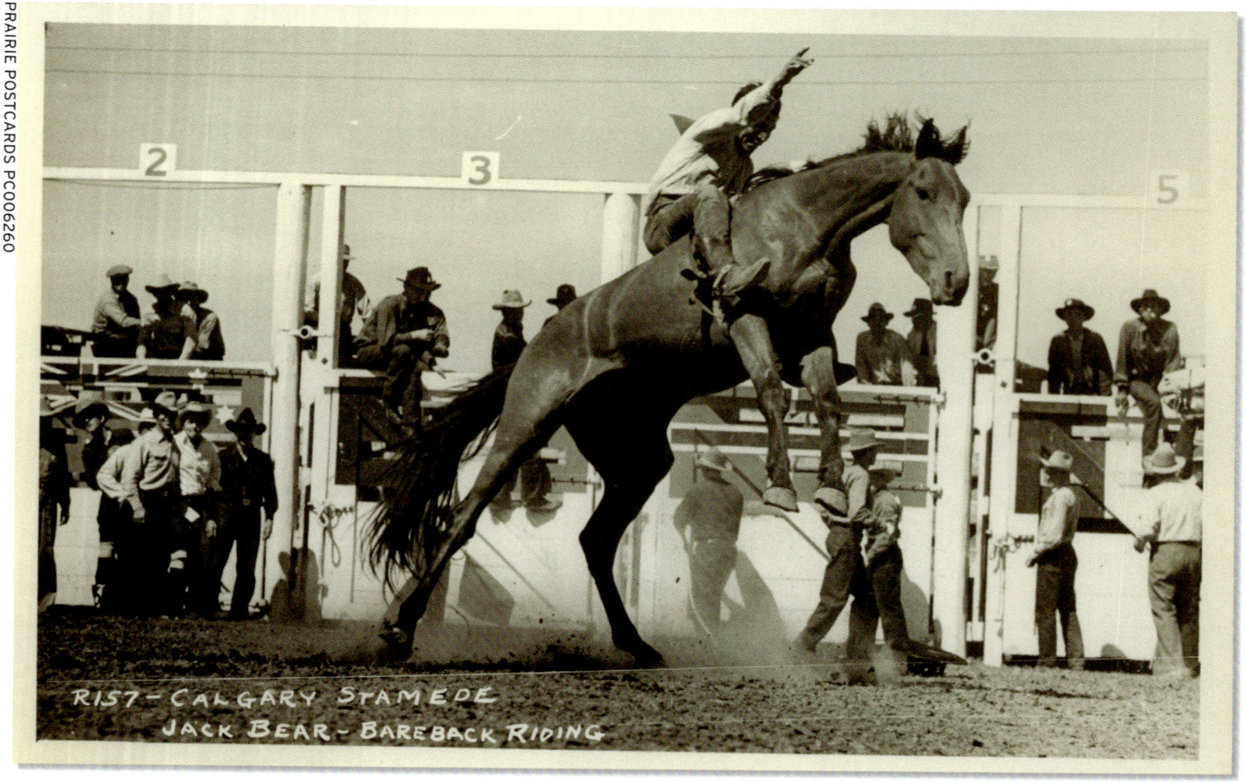

Jack Bear in the bareback bronc event at the Calgary Stampede, another Calgary Photo Supply Co. card

PRAIRIE POSTCARDS PC002247

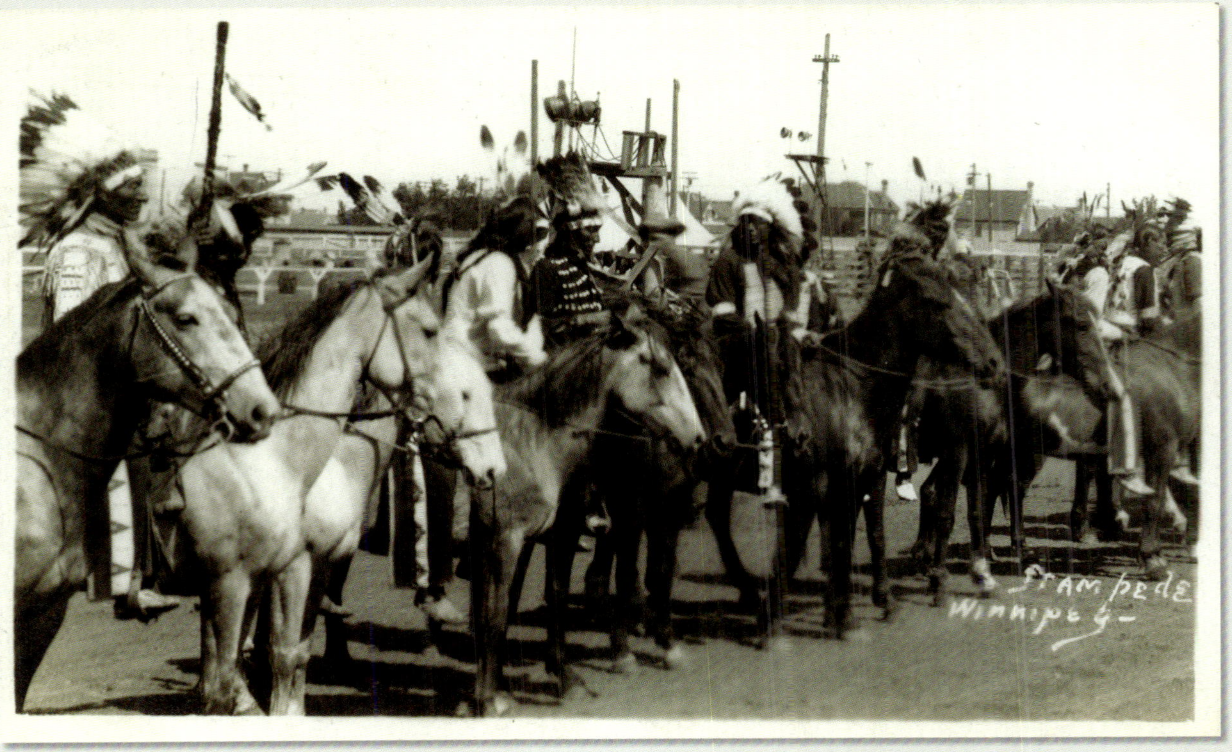

Aboriginal riders in full regalia prepare for the Winnipeg Stampede parade in 1913.

PRAIRIE POSTCARDS PC002172

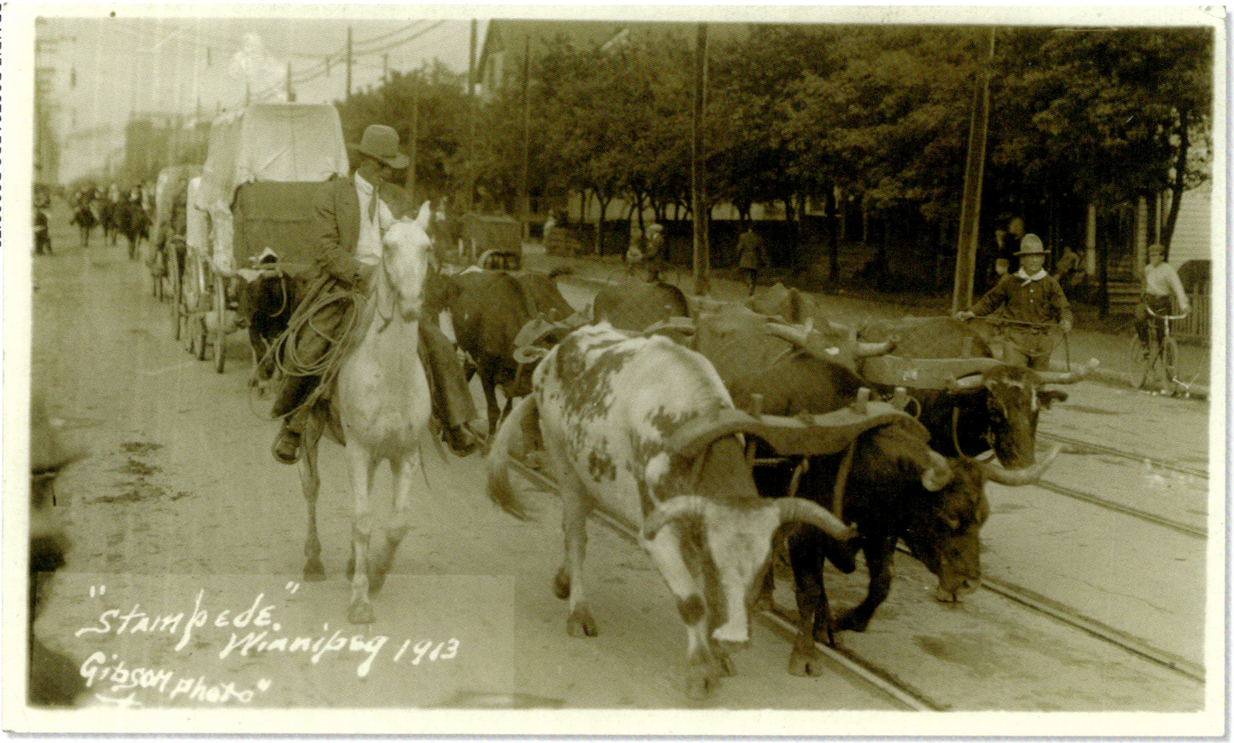

A Gibson Photo postcard showing the Winnipeg Stampede parade 1913. The bull team pulling three freight wagons was a valued symbol of the recently passed frontier days across the Canadian West.

PRAIRIE POSTCARDS PC002175

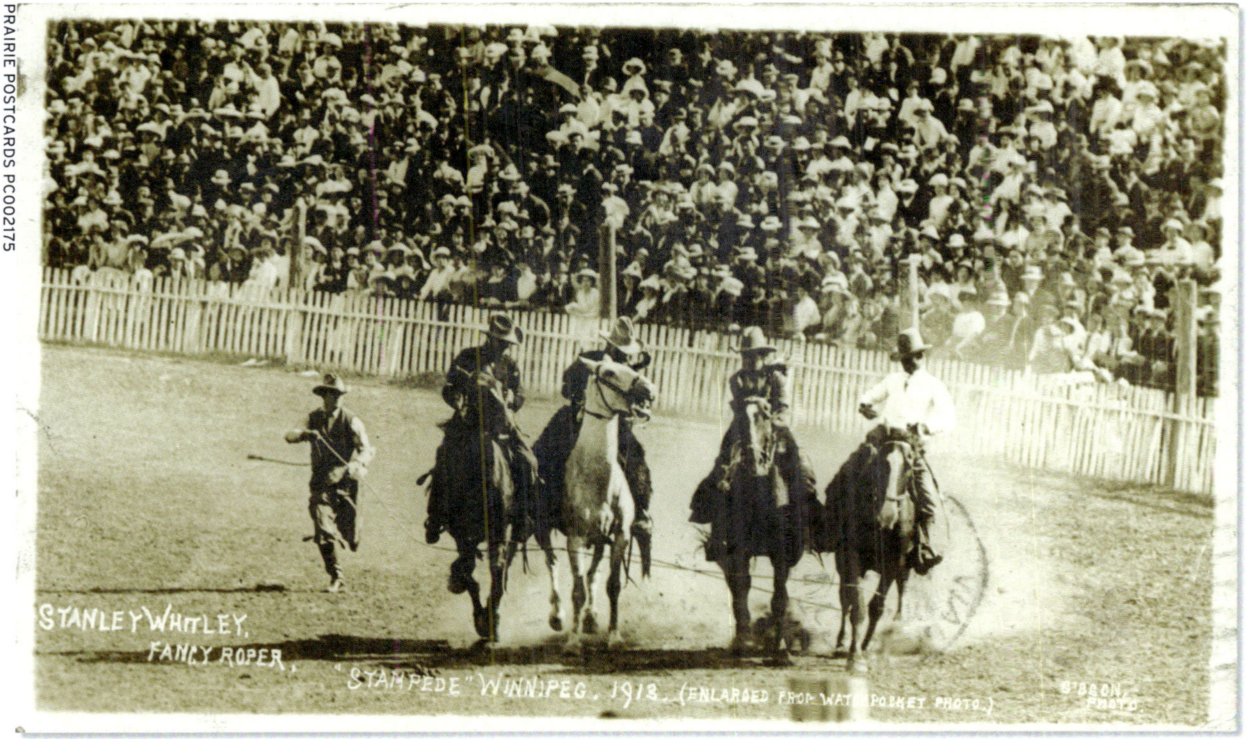

Stanley Whitley, fancy roper, demonstrates his skills in another Gibson Photo scene from the 1913 Winnipeg Stampede.

PRAIRIE POSTCARDS PC003715

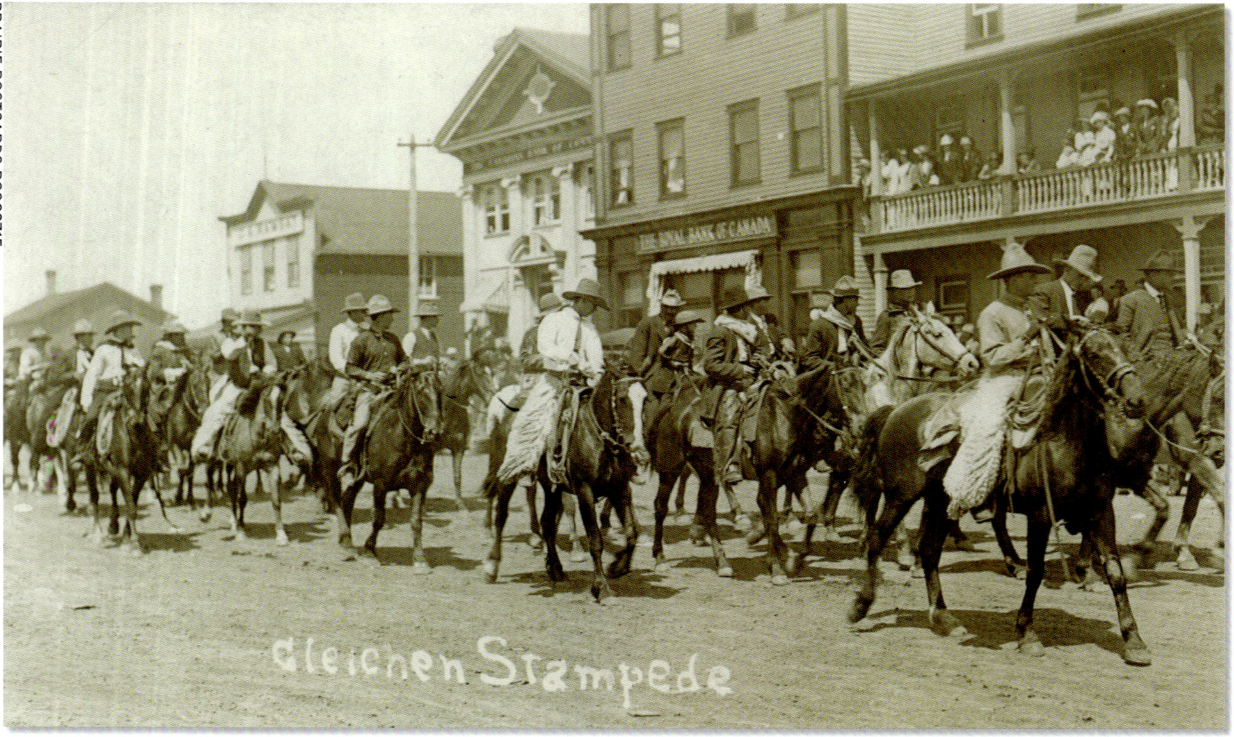

An early small-town parade delights the crowds at the Gleichen Stampede around 1915.

PRAIRIE POSTCARDS PC004451

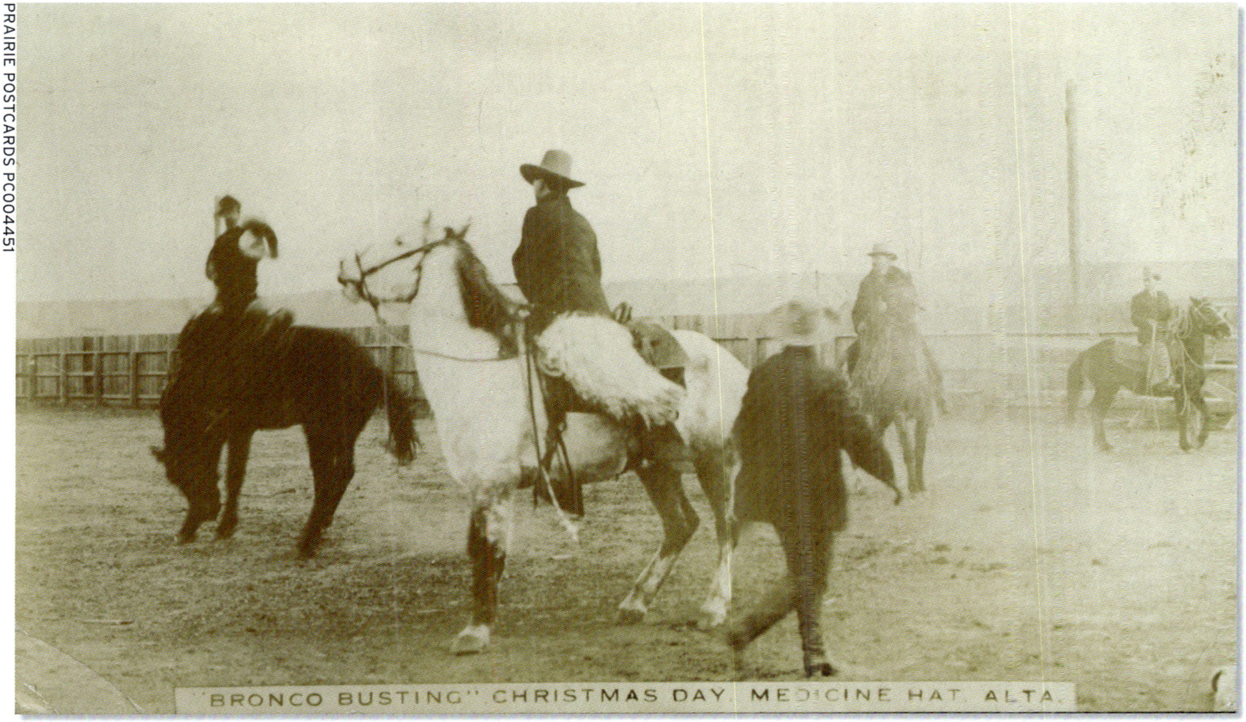

Not all rodeo events were held during stampedes. Here, cowboys ride bucking horses on Christmas Day 1914 at Medicine Hat, Alberta.

PRAIRIE POSTCARDS PC004244

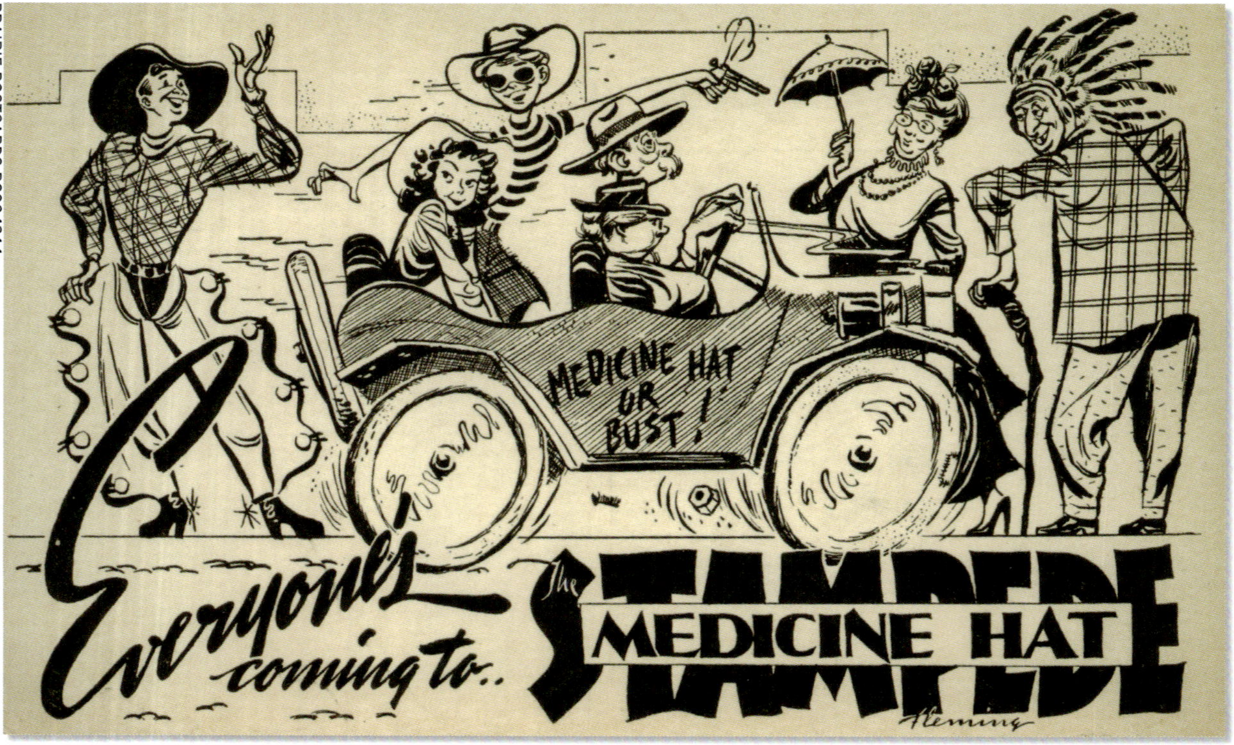

"Everyone's coming to the Medicine Hat Stampede," a 1950s Fleming Card promoting the event

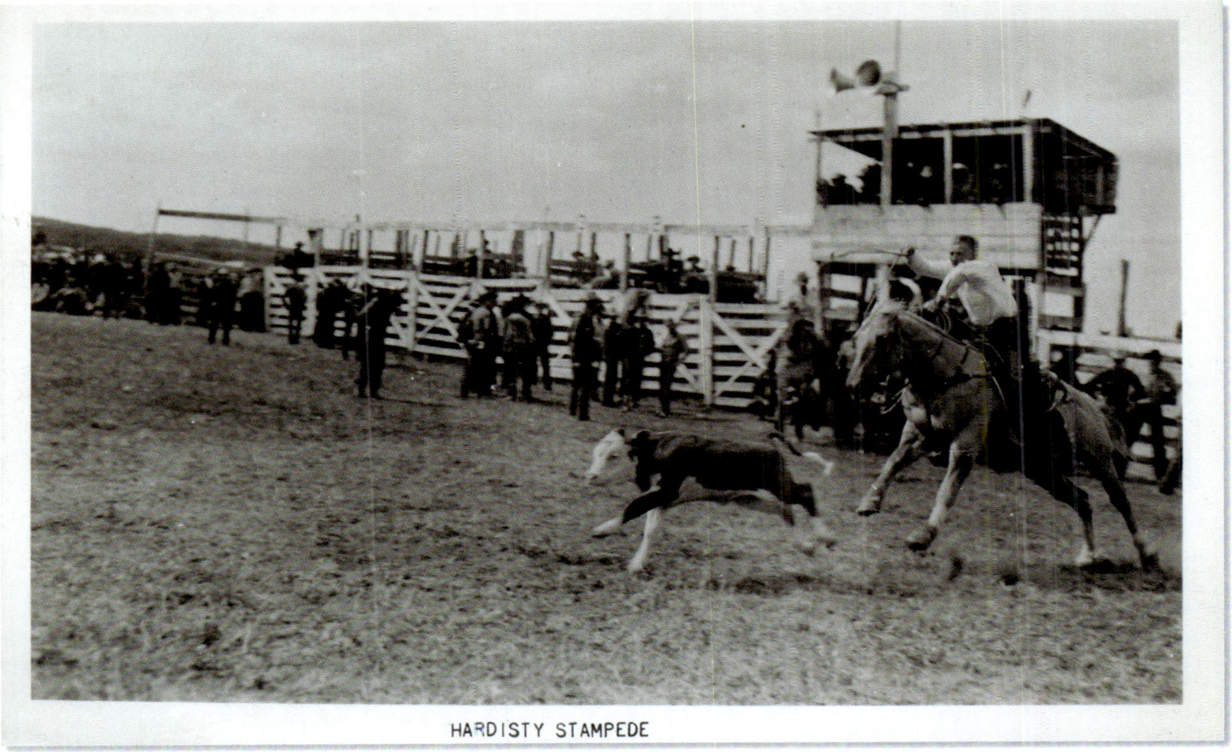

PRAIRIE POSTCARDS PC003768

Calf roping at the 1953 Hardisty Stampede. Established in 1948, just after the Second World War, the Hardisty Rodeo is still held each year.

PRAIRIE POSTCARDS PC005026

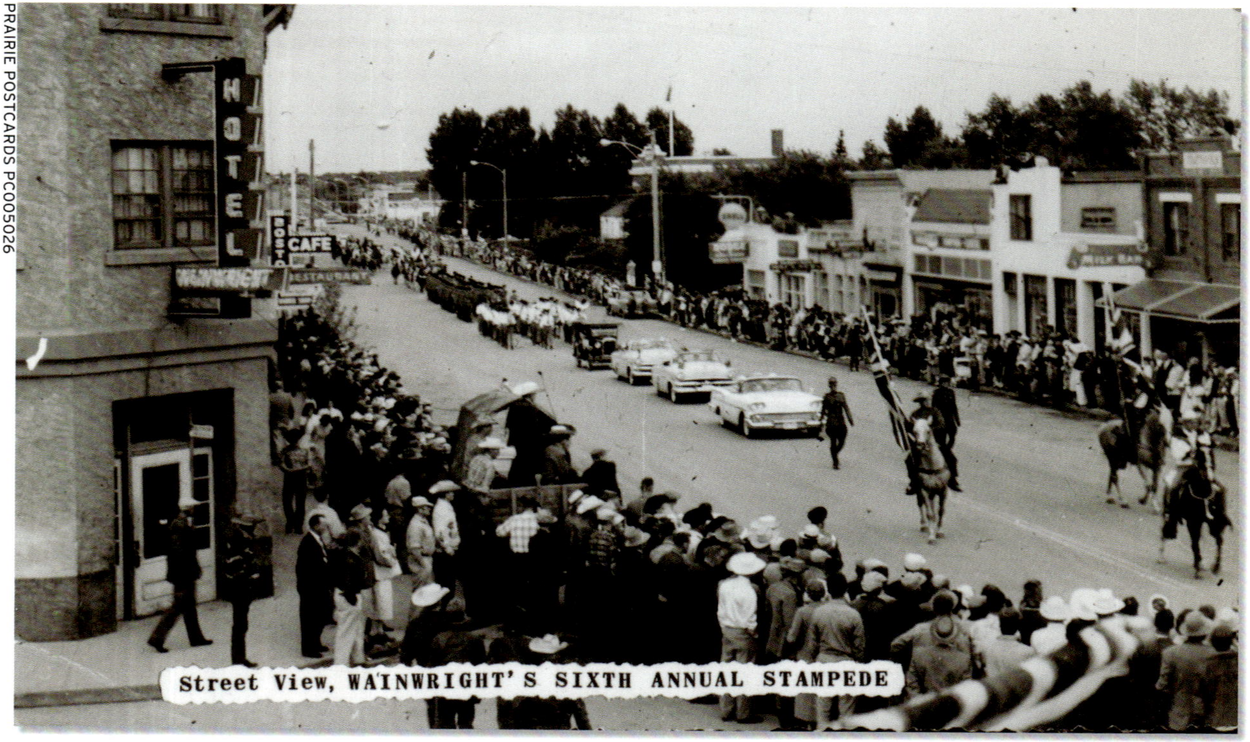

The Canadian Post Card Co. of Toronto captured the sixth annual Wainwright Stampede parade, held in 1958. This event continues to this day.

FURTHER READING

Barris, Ted, and Robert Semeniuk. *Rodeo Cowboys: The Last Heroes*. Edmonton: Executive Sport Publications, 1981.

Belanger, Art. *Chuckwagon Racing: Calgary Stampede's Half Mile of Hell*. Calgary and Surrey, BC: Frontier Books, 1970, 1984.

Bryden, Wendy. *The First Stampede of Flores LaDue: Based on the True Love Story of Florence and Guy Weadick in Celebration of the Centenary of the Calgary Stampede, 1912-2012*. 1st Touchstone export ed. New York: Simon & Schuster, 2011.

Dixon, Joan, and Tracey Read. *Celebrating the Calgary Exhibition & Stampede: The Story of the Greatest Outdoor Show on Earth*. Canmore, Alta.: Altitude Publishing Canada, 2005.

Foran, Max, ed. *Icon, Brand, Myth: The Calgary Exhibition & Stampede*. The West Unbound: Social & Cultural Studies series. Edmonton: AU Press, 2008.

Gray, James H. *A Brand of its Own: The 100 Year History of the Calgary Exhibition & Stampede*. Saskatoon: Western Producer Prairie Books, 1985.

Kennedy, Fred. *Calgary Stampede: The Authentic Story of the Calgary Exhibition & Stampede, "The Greatest Outdoor Show on Earth," 1912–1964*. Vancouver: West Vancouver Enterprises, 1965.

Livingstone, Donna. *The Cowboy Spirit: Guy Weadick and the Calgary Stampede*. Vancouver: Greystone Books, 1996.

Nelson, Doug. *Hotcakes to High Stakes: The Chuckwagon Story*. Calgary: Detselig, 1993.

Tivy, Patrick. *Calgary Stampede and the Canadian West*. Vancouver: Altitude Publishing Canada, 1995.

INDEX OF NAMES